T0215176

Exploring Windows Presentation Foundation

With Practical Applications in .NET 5

Taurius Litvinavicius

Apress®

Exploring Windows Presentation Foundation: With Practical Applications in .NET 5

Taurius Litvinavicius
Jonava, Lithuania

ISBN-13 (pbk): 978-1-4842-6636-6   ISBN-13 (electronic): 978-1-4842-6637-3
https://doi.org/10.1007/978-1-4842-6637-3

Copyright © 2021 by Taurius Litvinavicius

Managing Director, Apress Media LLC: Welmoed Spahr
Acquisitions Editor: Smriti Srivastava
Development Editor: Laura Berendson
Coordinating Editor: Shrikant Vishwakarma

Cover designed by eStudioCalamar

Cover image designed by Pexels

Distributed to the book trade worldwide by Springer Science+Business Media LLC, 1 New York Plaza, Suite 4600, New York, NY 10004. Phone 1-800-SPRINGER, fax (201) 348-4505, e-mail orders-ny@springer-sbm.com, or visit www.springeronline.com. Apress Media, LLC is a California LLC and the sole member (owner) is Springer Science + Business Media Finance Inc (SSBM Finance Inc). SSBM Finance Inc is a **Delaware** corporation.

For information on translations, please e-mail booktranslations@springernature.com; for reprint, paperback, or audio rights, please e-mail bookpermissions@springernature.com.

Apress titles may be purchased in bulk for academic, corporate, or promotional use. eBook versions and licenses are also available for most titles. For more information, reference our Print and eBook Bulk Sales web page at http://www.apress.com/bulk-sales.

Any source code or other supplementary material referenced by the author in this book is available to readers on GitHub via the book's product page, located at www.apress.com/978-1-4842-6636-6. For more detailed information, please visit http://www.apress.com/source-code.

Printed on acid-free paper

Table of Contents

About the Author vii

About the Technical Reviewer ix

Introduction xi

Chapter 1: Getting Started 1

  Button and Click Event 1

  Window and Page 6

  Text Box... 12

  Message Box... 14

  Quick Example 18

  Quick Exercise 22

Chapter 2: Events 33

  Application Events 33

  Mouse Events... 34

  Keyboard Events 38

  Window Events.. 39

  Quick Example 41

  Quick Exercise 44

Chapter 3: UI Elements 51

Progress Bar 51

Tabs 55

Radio Button 56

Check Box 59

Slider 62

Image 64

Media Element 65

Menu 70

List View 71

Web Browser 74

Canvas 75

Generate Elements in C# 78

Background Tasks 81

Chapter 4: Files 85

Pick and Save 85

Quick Example 89

Quick Exercise 95

Chapter 5: MVVM 101

Element to Element Binding 103

Introducing ViewModel 104

Implementing Models 109

Quick Example 116

Quick Exercise 136

Solution 141

Chapter 6: Styles **151**

Window Size and Other Sizes 151

Style 160

Quick Example 177

Quick Exercise 208

    Solution 210

Index...**223**

About the Author

Taurius Litvinavicius is a businessman and technology expert based in Lithuania who has worked with various organizations in building and implementing projects in software development, sales, and other fields of business. He is responsible for technological improvements, development of new features, and general management. Taurius is also the director at the Conficiens solutio consulting agency where he supervises the development and maintenance of various projects and activities.

About the Technical Reviewer

Carsten Thomsen is a back-end developer primarily but working with smaller front-end bits as well. He has authored and reviewed a number of books, and created numerous Microsoft Learning courses, all to do with software development. He works as a freelancer/contractor in various countries in Europe, using Azure, Visual Studio, Azure DevOps, and GitHub as some of his tools. Being an exceptional troubleshooter, asking the right questions, including the less logical ones, in a most logical to least logical fashion, he also enjoys working with architecture, research, analysis, development, testing, and bug fixing. Carsten is a very good communicator with great mentoring and team lead skills and great skills researching and presenting new material.

Introduction

In this book, you will find lots of information about Windows Presentation Foundation (WPF) which will help you get started with it. Alongside the explanations of features, you will find use case examples and exercise assignments for you to practice what you have learned.

The first chapter will provide you with a basic introduction to the WPF. That will include handling button click event, window handling, accessing text box inputs, and a few more things. In the next chapter, you will see some generic events; some of them are related to the window, some to the mouse, and some to other things. The third chapter will cover various UI elements in WPF; it will also be useful to you for future reference. It is important to read and understand the first chapter, but in case you are in a hurry, you may skip the second and third chapters and only use them as reference later.

The fourth chapter will show you how to handle files in the WPF interface, and with that, it will provide some use cases to study. At this point, the examples will incorporate quite a few items from the previous chapters. Then in the fifth, you will see how the MVVM structure can be implemented – the explanation will be a practical one; this should help you understand MVVM quicker. The final chapter will cover the styling aspects of WPF, but with that, it will also show examples that incorporate most things that you can find in the previous chapters. Once again, if you are rushing to get started with WPF and do not have too much time, you may skip the MVVM chapter. But it would be a good idea to take a look at it later, as it is useful to understand what MVVM is and how it is implemented.

CHAPTER 1

Getting Started

Windows Presentation Foundation (WPF) has many features and many
arrangements you can choose from, but there are a few crucial things that
you have to know before going anywhere else. For any user interaction
to be viable in WPF, you need to understand how to use the methods,
and with that, you also need to understand how to set properties on the
elements. In this chapter, we will begin with only a handful of them, and in
Chapter 3, you will see many more to choose from, and they function in a
very similar way. Before going further, you should also understand how to
establish and then display or close windows and how to display quick and
simple alert messages.

Button and Click Event

Probably the most important element in WPF is the button, and probably
the most important event is the click event. Now, the main three things in
WPF are elements (e.g., button), events, and names of the elements. The
first thing you will learn about is a button, but for it to make sense, you will
also need to look at something called text block and label.

© Taurius Litvinavicius 2021
T. Litvinavicius, *Exploring Windows Presentation Foundation*,
https://doi.org/10.1007/978-1-4842-6637-3_1

Figure 1-1. *File layout in the project*

To begin with, we will work with the MainWindow.xaml source file, which is where the XAML code for the window and its elements go (Figure 1-1). MainWindow.xaml.cs is what is called a code-behind file; that is where the C# code for that window goes. In the next section, you will learn how to add more windows and navigate between them.

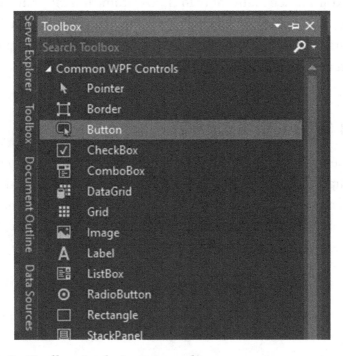

Figure 1-2. *Toolbox in design view editor*

Once you get into the MainWindow.xaml code, you will see a designer view. Although you can set various properties in XAML, it is best to drag and drop from the toolbox (Figure 1-2) and then move things around, expand them, and do other things in the designer. Once you drag and drop something onto the designer view, the XAML code for that element will be generated.

Figure 1-3. *Window view for the example*

This is what our example (see Figure 1-3) will look like (after the buttons are clicked).

Listing 1-1. XAML code for the MainWindow.xaml

```
<Window x:Class="WpfApp3.MainWindow"
        xmlns="http://schemas.microsoft.com/winfx/2006/xaml/
        presentation"
        xmlns:x="http://schemas.microsoft.com/winfx/2006/xaml"
        xmlns:d="http://schemas.microsoft.com/expression/
        blend/2008"
        xmlns:mc="http://schemas.openxmlformats.org/markup-
        compatibility/2006"
```

3

```
        xmlns:local="clr-namespace:WpfApp3"
        mc:Ignorable="d"
        Title="MainWindow" Height="450" Width="800">
    <Grid>
        <Button x:Name="bt1" Content="first option"
        HorizontalAlignment="Left" Margin="350,163,0,0"
        VerticalAlignment="Top" Width="101"/>
        <TextBlock x:Name="textblock1"
        HorizontalAlignment="Left" Margin="350,198,0,0"
        TextWrapping="Wrap" VerticalAlignment="Top"
        Width="101"/>

        <Button Click="Button_Click" Content="second option"
        HorizontalAlignment="Left" Margin="350,229,0,0"
        VerticalAlignment="Top" Width="101"/>
        <Label x:Name="label1" Content=""
        HorizontalAlignment="Left" Margin="350,254,0,0"
        VerticalAlignment="Top" Width="101"/>
    </Grid>
</Window>
```

This is the XAML code (Listing 1-1) for MainWindow.xaml; all the elements go into the Grid element. The first element in the grid is a Button. In it, we have a name property (you will see why we need it in the C# code); after that, we have Content, which is the text displayed in the button. After that, two very important properties are HorizontalAlignment and VerticalAlignment, which are important because they determine the alignment, and with that, you can use margins accordingly.

The next element is the TextBlock which is used to display text – the crucial part here is the name, as that will be the reference point in C#. With that, you can also see TextWrapping – if set, it will wrap the text onto a new line; if not set, the default value will be used (NoWrap) and the text will be displayed in a single line.

Another Button, similar to the first one, but with no name specified. Instead, we have the Click property which has a value of Button_Click – this will correspond with the event method name in C#. So, you will basically see two ways of declaring an event.

Finally, we have a label, which is an element very similar to a TextBlock. But the label has fewer options in terms of customization.

Listing 1-2. C# code for MainWindow.xaml.cs

```
public partial class MainWindow : Window
    {
        public MainWindow()
        {
            InitializeComponent();
            bt1.Click += Bt1_Click;
        }

        private void Bt1_Click(object sender, RoutedEventArgs e)
        {
            textblock1.Text = "button works 1";
        }

        private void Button_Click(object sender,
        RoutedEventArgs e)
        {
            label1.Content = "button works 2";
        }
    }
```

In the C# code (code-behind) (see Listing 1-2), you can first see the constructor method for the window class. In it, we declare the button click event for the first button. In the code, the first event is for the first button and the second for the second button. To set a display value for the TextBlock, you need to set the Text property, but for the label, you set the Content property.

Window and Page

In WPF there are two main view options – one is window, and the other is page. Another option may be tabs, or you may simply change visibility of grids and other containers, but that will be covered in the next chapters (Chapters 3 and 6).

Both window and page will have XAML part and C# part (code-behind). The main difference is how they are displayed and how the user navigates between them.

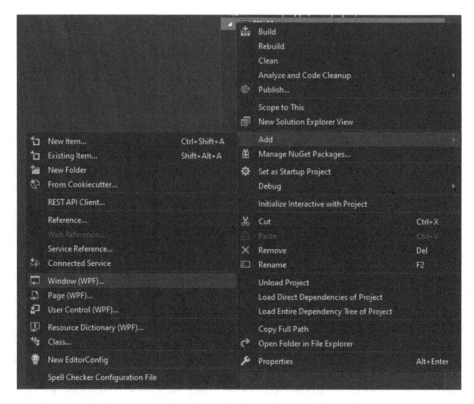

Figure 1-4. *Adding Window file in WPF project*

To create a new window, you need to right-click your project (or folder in which you will place the file) and then go to add and choose Window (WPF) (see Figure 1-4). Alternatively, you can find this option in "New Item".

Listing 1-3. XAML code in MainWindow.xaml

```
<Window x:Class="WpfApp.MainWindow"
        xmlns="http://schemas.microsoft.com/winfx/2006/xaml/
        presentation"
        xmlns:x="http://schemas.microsoft.com/winfx/2006/xaml"
        xmlns:d="http://schemas.microsoft.com/expression/
        blend/2008"
        xmlns:mc="http://schemas.openxmlformats.org/markup-
        compatibility/2006"
        xmlns:local="clr-namespace:WpfApp"
        mc:Ignorable="d"
        Title="MainWindow" Height="450" Width="800">
    <Grid>
        <Button x:Name="bt1" Content="window 1"
        HorizontalAlignment="Left" Margin="246,118,0,0"
        VerticalAlignment="Top" Width="75"/>

    </Grid>
</Window>
```

The XAML part of a window (See Listing 1-3) will contain all the markup for your elements and the window itself. By default, a window will contain a grid and that is where you should place your elements – you cannot do that in the window itself. In the default window, everything from x:Class to mc:Ignorable should not be modified; otherwise, it may break. You may change the title property (which appears at the top-left corner of a window), and you can change the height and width properties. There are many more things that you can do with a window, and some of them will be covered in the last chapter of this book.

Listing 1-4. MainWindow.xaml.cs contents

```
public MainWindow()
        {
            InitializeComponent();
            bt1.Click += Bt1_Click;

        }

        private void Bt1_Click(object sender, RoutedEventArgs e)
        {
            Window w1 = new Window1();
            w1.Show();
        }
```

By default, the application will open your main window (MainWindow), but later, you can close it and/or open more windows, and there are two ways of doing this. In this particular example, we have another window created, and it is named Window1. You can see that on button click event (see Listing 1-4), we construct and establish a variable for that new window. To display it, we execute the **Show** method. This will display the new window, but it will not close the existing one and will allow to interact with the existing window. An alternative to that is to open a window by using the ShowDialog method; this will freeze the existing window and will only allow the user to interact with the new one. To close the current window, you will need to use the **this.Close()** method or you can control by reference; in this case, it would be **w1.Close()**.

It is also important to understand the constructor method for the window. By default, you have the InitializeComponent method which initializes all the elements declared in the window. So, if you want to set properties (e.g., set text to text block), you need to do all that after InitializeComponent has occurred.

The Page is not as stand-alone as a Window; instead, you use pages to establish some navigation inside a Window.

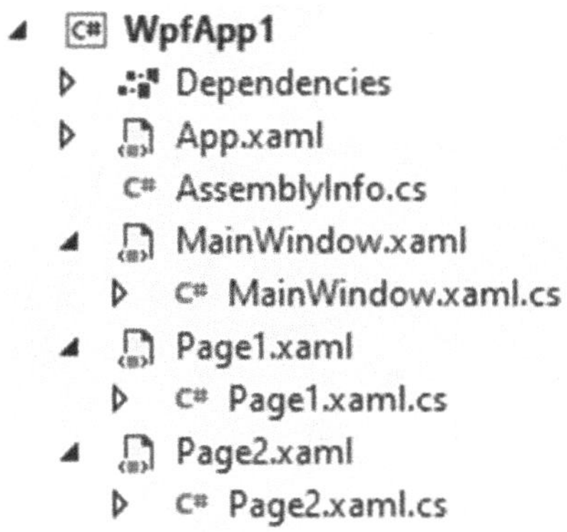

WpfApp1
Dependencies
App.xaml
AssemblyInfo.cs
MainWindow.xaml
MainWindow.xaml.cs
Page1.xaml
Page1.xaml.cs
Page2.xaml
Page2.xaml.cs

Figure 1-5. *File layout in the project*

In this example, we have added two new files (see Figure 1-5) – Pages.

MainWindow
To page 1
To page 2

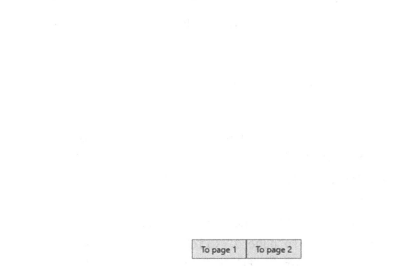

Figure 1-6. *First state of the view (nothing clicked)*

Initially, you will see an empty window like this (Figure 1-6).

Figure 1-7. *Second state of the view ("To page 1" button clicked)*

After the button is clicked, a page will be displayed (see Figure 1-7). If the second button is clicked, the first page will be replaced with the second one.

Listing 1-5. MainWindow.xaml contents

```
<Grid>
        <Frame x:Name="fr"    Margin="0,0,0,66" NavigationUI
        Visibility="Hidden"/>
        <Button Content="To page 1" Click="Button_Click"
        HorizontalAlignment="Left" Margin="321,406,0,0"
        VerticalAlignment="Top" Height="28" Width="79"/>
        <Button Content="To page 2" Click="Button_Click_1"
        HorizontalAlignment="Left" Margin="400,406,0,0"
        VerticalAlignment="Top" Height="28" Width="79"/>
    </Grid>
```

In your window (see Listing 1-5) in which you want to display pages, you will need a Frame element – that is where a page is displayed. You need to set an appropriate size, establish a name, and then set NavigationUIVisibility to Hidden. The last one is not important from a functional perspective, but if not set, it would display a navigation bar, similar to what a browser might have.

Listing 1-6. Events in MainWindow.xaml.cs

```
private void Button_Click(object sender, RoutedEventArgs e)
      {
          fr.Content = new Page1();
      }

      private void Button_Click_1(object sender,
      RoutedEventArgs e)
      {
          fr.Content = new Page2();
      }
```

Navigating to a page is quite simple here (See Listing 1-6); you just need to set the Content property of the Frame element.

Listing 1-7. Constructor method for Page1 (Page1.xaml.cs)

```
public Page1()
      {
          InitializeComponent();
      }
```

A Page has a constructor (see Listing 1-7) just like a Window, and inside that, you will find the same arrangement with the InitializeComponent method.

Text Box

There are two basic interactive elements in WPF – the first one you already know, which is a button, and the second one is the text box. In this book, you will see more elements in the third chapter, but this will be your starting point in understanding the input elements.

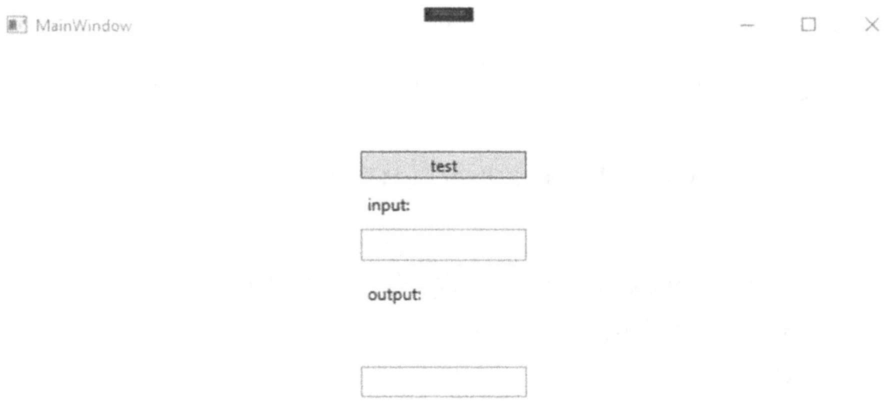

Figure 1-8. *Window view for the example*

Listing 1-8. MainWindow.xaml contents

```
<Grid>
        <Label Content="input:" HorizontalAlignment="Left"
        Margin="328,100,0,0" VerticalAlignment="Top"
        Width="106"/>
        <TextBox x:Name="tb1" HorizontalAlignment="Left"
        Height="23" Margin="328,131,0,0" TextWrapping="Wrap"
        VerticalAlignment="Top" Width="120"/>
        <Label Content="output:" HorizontalAlignment="Left"
        Margin="328,164,0,0" VerticalAlignment="Top"
        Width="106"/>
```

```
    <TextBox x:Name="output2" HorizontalAlignment="Left"
    Height="22" Margin="328,230,0,0" TextWrapping="Wrap"
    VerticalAlignment="Top" Width="120"/>
    <Label x:Name="output1" Content=""
    HorizontalAlignment="Left" Margin="328,199,0,0"
    VerticalAlignment="Top" Width="106"/>
    <Button Click="Button_Click" Content="test"
    HorizontalAlignment="Left" Margin="328,75,0,0"
    VerticalAlignment="Top" Width="120"/>
</Grid>
```

In this case, we have six elements (see Figure 1-8 and Listing 1-8) in the XAML (the grid is in the window). The first label simply has some static text, the second element is a text box, and a text box needs a name for referencing in C#. After that, we have another static label and then we have another text box with a name. There is also another label with a name (it will be used from C#) and finally a button with an event. Notice, in this case, the event is declared in XAML; therefore, you will not see it declared in the C# code. The idea here is to enter something into the input box (tb1) and output the value in the label (output1) and text box (output2).

If you want to have multiple lines in your text box input, you need to set the AcceptsReturn property to True. Also, by default, the text box does not accept tab input; if you want that, you will need to set AcceptsTab="True".

Listing 1-9. Button click event

```
private void Button_Click(object sender, RoutedEventArgs e)
        {
            output1.Content = tb1.Text + " 1";
            output2.Text = tb1.Text + " 2";
        }
```

This is the event on button click in the C# part (see Listing 1-9). Now, the output1 is a label and a label has the property Content, which is what you assign to display something. On the other hand, text box has the Text property, which will hold the input and can also be assigned to display something. The most important thing in any input element is to know which property holds the value – in this case, it is quite easy to find, but later, you will see some elements that are a bit more tricky.

Message Box

Message box is a great way to display basic notifications and alerts to the user; it is simple to use and can be a great safeguard on some occasions. Now, we will look at how it is implemented, but before that, you have to know about the possible arrangements of this feature. There are four default options in a message in terms of the buttons it may contain. Each button, when clicked, will close the box and return a result (MessageBoxResult). Later in this book, you will learn how to make your own custom message box (refer to Chapter 6).

Figure 1-9. *Simple message box*

The first variation (see Figure 1-9) is a message box with an OK button. This option should not be used to return a value, as there is only one option for that. However, this would be the most commonly used option, as it is best for displaying simple warnings (e.g., wrong password, disconnected).

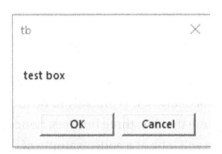

Figure 1-10. *OK/Cancel message box*

This option (see Figure 1-10) is best for when the user has to leave (or clear) something. In those arrangements, this would be the last chance for them to avoid data loss.

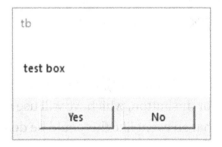

Figure 1-11. *Yes/No message box*

The Yes/No option (see Figure 1-11) is very similar to OK/Cancel, as it can be used for the same purposes (e.g., "Do you want to leave this window?"). However, the return values will be different.

15

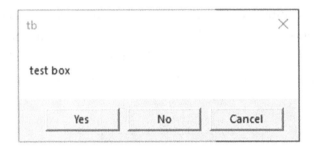

Figure 1-12. *Yes/No/Cancel message box*

The final option (see Figure 1-12) is the most elaborate one, and it can be used in various scenarios. It is unlikely to be the most common type, but it is the only one that has three buttons, hence three different possible outcomes. We will look at a code example of this message box implemented.

Listing 1-10. XAML code in MainWindow.xaml

```xaml
<Grid>
        <Button x:Name="mbtestbt" Content="test"
        HorizontalAlignment="Left" Margin="360,179,0,0"
        VerticalAlignment="Top" Width="75"/>

    </Grid>
```

In the XAML part (See Listing 1-10), we only have one button defined. We also have a name for the button, which we will use to establish an event. Do remember that an event like this could be defined on the button in the XAML.

Listing 1-11. Contents of MainWindow.xaml.cs

```
public MainWindow()
        {
            InitializeComponent();
            mbtestbt.Click += Mbtestbt_Click;
        }

        private void Mbtestbt_Click(object sender,
        RoutedEventArgs e)
        {
            MessageBoxResult mbresult = MessageBox.Show("test
            box", "tb", MessageBoxButton.YesNoCancel);
             MessageBox.Show(mbresult.ToString());
            if (MessageBoxResult.Yes == mbresult)
            {
                MessageBox.Show("yes clicked!");
            }
        }
```

In the window class constructor (see Listing 1-11), we establish our click event, and the event is where the interesting part begins. First, we need to show the message box, and that is done using MessageBox.Show, which in this case has a return value – MessageBoxResult. The **Show** method has other variations as well, and it does not have to return a value to be used; it also does not have to specify other values. In this example, we actually display the result that user chose, and then you can see an if statement where we check for result values being **Yes**.

Quick Example

To wrap things up with the basics, we have a very basic example. This will show you how some of these elements and feature of WPF can interact together.

Figure 1-13. *The window view for the example*

As you can see (see Figure 1-13), we have a simple registration form. We will not look at the full functionality of such an arrangement, but you will see how these elements can work to create something useful. The Generate button will generate a five-digit password, and the Copy button will copy it to the clipboard. On the Submit button, we do send the data anywhere, but we do check for the password to be longer than three characters (i.e., at least four characters).

Listing 1-12. Contents of MainWindow.xaml in the example

```
<Window x:Class="WpfApp1.MainWindow"
        xmlns="http://schemas.microsoft.com/winfx/2006/xaml/
        presentation"
        xmlns:x="http://schemas.microsoft.com/winfx/2006/xaml"
        xmlns:d="http://schemas.microsoft.com/expression/
        blend/2008"
        xmlns:mc="http://schemas.openxmlformats.org/markup-
        compatibility/2006"
        xmlns:local="clr-namespace:WpfApp1"
        mc:Ignorable="d"
        Title="Registration window" Height="450" Width="415">
    <Grid HorizontalAlignment="Center" Width="415">
        <Label Content="Full name" HorizontalAlignment="Center"
        Margin="0,62,0,0" VerticalAlignment="Top" Width="147"/>
        <TextBox x:Name="tb_fullname"
        HorizontalAlignment="Left" Margin="134,93,0,0"
        TextWrapping="Wrap" VerticalAlignment="Top"
        Width="120"/>
        <Label Content="Email" HorizontalAlignment="Center"
        Margin="0,136,0,0" VerticalAlignment="Top"
        Width="147"/>
        <TextBox x:Name="tb_email" HorizontalAlignment="Left"
        Margin="134,167,0,0" TextWrapping="Wrap"
        VerticalAlignment="Top" Width="120"/>
```

```xaml
<Label Content="Password" HorizontalAlignment="Center"
Margin="0,207,0,0" VerticalAlignment="Top"
Width="147"/>
<TextBox x:Name="tb_password"
HorizontalAlignment="Left" Margin="134,238,0,0"
TextWrapping="Wrap" VerticalAlignment="Top"
Width="120"/>
<Button x:Name="bt_copy" Click="bt_copy_Click"
Content="Copy" HorizontalAlignment="Left"
Margin="254,238,0,0" VerticalAlignment="Top" Width="61"
Padding="0" Height="18"/>
<Button x:Name="bt_generate" Click="bt_generate_
Click" Content="Generate" HorizontalAlignment="Left"
Margin="158,261,0,0" VerticalAlignment="Top" Width="75"
Height="19"/>
<Button x:Name="bt_submit" Click="bt_submit_
Click" Content="Submit" HorizontalAlignment="Left"
Margin="158,335,0,0" VerticalAlignment="Top" Width="76"
Height="18"/>

    </Grid>
</Window>
```

The first thing you may notice in the XAML code (See Listing 1-12) is the window title, and then you can see that the width is set to 415. The labels in this case are simply for displaying static values. After that, notice how the text boxes and buttons are named. The text boxes start with **tb**, and the buttons start with **bt**; this helps when you have to type in the names in the C# code. Also, when you have a name for the button and create an event through XAML, a very appropriate name for the event will be generated.

Listing 1-13. MainWindow.xaml.cs contents

```
public MainWindow()
        {
            InitializeComponent();
        }

        private void bt_copy_Click(object sender,
        RoutedEventArgs e)
        {
            Clipboard.SetText(tb_password.Text);
        }

        private void bt_generate_Click(object sender,
        RoutedEventArgs e)
        {
            var rnd = new Random();
            tb_password.Text = rnd.Next(20000, 30000).ToString();
        }

        private void bt_submit_Click(object sender,
        RoutedEventArgs e)
        {
            if (tb_password.Text.Length < 4)
            {
                MessageBox.Show("Password needs to be at least
                4 characters.", "Password error");
                return;
            }

            //submit
        }
```

As you can see, we do not have any code in the window constructor; the button events are declared in XAML. The next thing you can look at is the bt_generate_Click event; the event itself is part of the WPF button, but everything in it is general C#. The bt_copy_Click event is a bit different; although some clipboard interactions are possible in other C# interface technologies, some of them might be a bit different from the others. You may also notice that in this case we retrieve value from the tb_password text property. Finally, the bt_submit_Click combines a few things covered in this chapter. First of all, we access the text property tb_password, and from there, we get the length property where we determine how many characters the password contains. After that, we use a basic message box to display the error message. A message box displayed this way will only contain the OK button. With all that, notice that after the message box, we have an empty return; this is very important because in full arrangement the next step in such flow would likely be something that should not happen if this error occurs.

Quick Exercise

Your task is to write an area calculator program, with three options – rectangle area, triangle area, and trapezoid area.

```
Rectangle area formula = a * b
Where a - base a, b - base b
Triangle area formula = a * h * 0.5
Where b - base, h - height
Trapezoid area formula = (a + b) / 2 * h
Where a - base a, b - base b, h - height
```

Each calculator should have its own separate view, and there should also be a main view from which the user could navigate to each calculator.

In the example for how this exercise may be completed, you will see an arrangement of three windows, each containing one type of calculator.

Figure 1-14. *File layout for example project*

In the project, you can see three new windows added (see Figure 1-14) – one for each calculator.

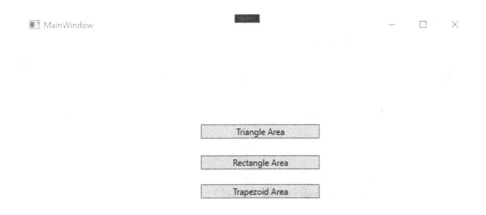

Figure 1-15. *Window view for the example*

Listing 1-14. XAML code for the MainWindow.xaml

```xml
<Grid>
        <Button x:Name="ToTriangle"  Click="ToTriangle_Click"
        Content="Triangle Area" HorizontalAlignment="Left"
        Margin="326,126,0,0" VerticalAlignment="Top"
        Width="170"/>
        <Button x:Name="ToTrapezoid" Click="ToTrapezoid_Click"
        Content="Trapezoid Area" HorizontalAlignment="Left"
        Margin="326,211,0,0" VerticalAlignment="Top"
        Width="170"/>
        <Button x:Name="ToRectangle" Click="ToRectangle_Click"
        Content="Rectangle Area" HorizontalAlignment="Left"
        Margin="326,170,0,0" VerticalAlignment="Top"
        Width="170"/>
</Grid>
```

In the main window, we have three buttons which when clicked will open windows containing calculators.

Listing 1-15. C# code for the MainWindow.xaml.cs

```csharp
private void ToTriangle_Click(object sender, RoutedEventArgs e)
        {
            TriangleAreaWindow triangleAreaWindow = new
            TriangleAreaWindow();
            triangleAreaWindow.Show();
        }

        private void ToTrapezoid_Click(object sender,
        RoutedEventArgs e)
        {
            TrapezoidAreaWindow trapezoidAreaWindow = new
            TrapezoidAreaWindow();
```

```
        trapezoidAreaWindow.Show();
    }

    private void ToRectangle_Click(object sender,
    RoutedEventArgs e)
    {
        RectangleAreaWindow rectangleAreaWindow = new
        RectangleAreaWindow();
        rectangleAreaWindow.Show();
    }
```

We then have three events (see Listing 1-15) for three buttons, and they all open new window accordingly.

Figure 1-16. *Window view for triangle area calculator*

Listing 1-16. XAML code in the TriangleAreaWindow.xaml

```
<Grid>
        <TextBlock HorizontalAlignment="Left"
        Margin="294,170,0,0" TextWrapping="Wrap" Text="a:"
        VerticalAlignment="Top" Width="16"/>
```

```
<TextBox x:Name="a_input" HorizontalAlignment="Left"
Height="16" Margin="315,170,0,0" TextWrapping="Wrap"
VerticalAlignment="Top" Width="83"/>
<TextBlock HorizontalAlignment="Left"
Margin="422,169,0,0" TextWrapping="Wrap" Text="b:"
VerticalAlignment="Top" Width="16"/>
<TextBox x:Name="b_input" HorizontalAlignment="Left"
Height="16" Margin="443,169,0,0" TextWrapping="Wrap"
VerticalAlignment="Top" Width="83"/>
<TextBlock HorizontalAlignment="Left"
Margin="294,89,0,0" TextWrapping="Wrap" Text="A =a * b"
VerticalAlignment="Top" Width="144"/>
<TextBlock HorizontalAlignment="Left"
Margin="131,170,0,0" TextWrapping="Wrap" Text="A ="
VerticalAlignment="Top" Width="25"/>
<TextBlock x:Name="A_output" HorizontalAlignment="Left"
Margin="161,170,0,0" TextWrapping="Wrap"
VerticalAlignment="Top" Width="44"/>
<Button Content="Calculate" HorizontalAlignment="Left"
Margin="24,171,0,0" VerticalAlignment="Top" Width="75"
Click="Button_Click"/>
</Grid>
```

From the window view (see Figure 1-16, Figure 1-15), it may not seem like we have a lot going on in the triangle area calculator, but then if you look at the XAML code (Listing 1-16), it will be a different story. But the main reason is because we have lots of text blocks to describe what is happening in the window. Other than that, we have text boxes for input and a button and also one TextBlock element for output.

Listing 1-17. Event for calculation button click

```
private void Button_Click(object sender, RoutedEventArgs e)
    {
        try
        {
            A_output.Text = (Convert.ToDouble(a_input.Text) *
            Convert.ToDouble(h_input.Text) / 2).ToString();
        }
        catch (Exception ex)
        {
            A_output.Text = "N/A";
        }
    }
```

In the C# code, we only have one event. It performs the calculation and applies the value to the Text property of output TextBlock element. The first thing to note here is the conversion from string to double – this is very important as the type for the Text property is string. We also have a try/catch statement, and those are quite important to have in any WPF application.

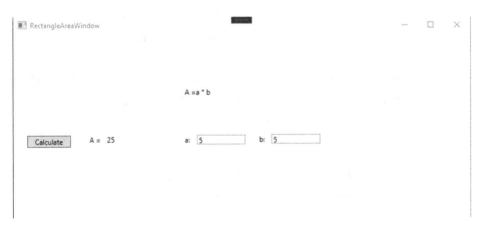

Figure 1-17. *Window view for rectangle area calculator*

Listing 1-18. RectangleAreaWindow.xaml contents

```
<Grid>
        <TextBlock HorizontalAlignment="Left"
        Margin="294,170,0,0" TextWrapping="Wrap" Text="a:"
        VerticalAlignment="Top" Width="16"/>
        <TextBox x:Name="a_input" HorizontalAlignment="Left"
        Height="16" Margin="315,170,0,0" TextWrapping="Wrap"
        VerticalAlignment="Top" Width="83"/>
        <TextBlock HorizontalAlignment="Left"
        Margin="422,169,0,0" TextWrapping="Wrap" Text="b:"
        VerticalAlignment="Top" Width="16"/>
        <TextBox x:Name="b_input" HorizontalAlignment="Left"
        Height="16" Margin="443,169,0,0" TextWrapping="Wrap"
        VerticalAlignment="Top" Width="83"/>
        s<TextBlock HorizontalAlignment="Left"
        Margin="294,89,0,0" TextWrapping="Wrap" Text="A =a * b"
        VerticalAlignment="Top" Width="144"/>
        <TextBlock HorizontalAlignment="Left"
        Margin="131,170,0,0" TextWrapping="Wrap" Text="A ="
        VerticalAlignment="Top" Width="25"/>
        <TextBlock x:Name="A_output" HorizontalAlignment="Left"
        Margin="161,170,0,0" TextWrapping="Wrap"
        VerticalAlignment="Top" Width="44"/>
        <Button  Content="Calculate" HorizontalAlignment="Left"
        Margin="24,171,0,0" VerticalAlignment="Top" Width="75"
        Click="Button_Click"/>
</Grid>
```

The rectangle calculator is quite similar (see Figure 1-17); we have inputs, we have formula displayed, and then we have a button.

Listing 1-19. Button click event for calculation

```
private void Button_Click(object sender, RoutedEventArgs e)
        {
            try
            {
                A_output.Text = (Convert.ToDouble(a_input.Text) *
                Convert.ToDouble(b_input.Text)).ToString();
            }
            catch (Exception ex)
            {
                A_output.Text = "N/A";
            }
        }
```

The C# part (see Listing 1-19) is again almost identical to the previous calculator; the only difference here is the formula used.

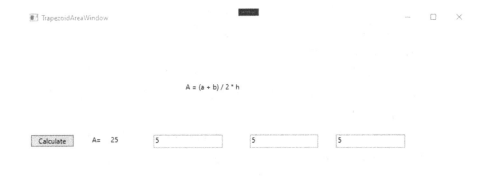

Figure 1-18. *Window view for trapezoid area calculator*

Listing 1-20. TrapezoidAreaWindow.xaml contents

```
<Grid>
        <TextBox x:Name="a_input" HorizontalAlignment="Left"
        Height="23" Margin="394,187,0,0" TextWrapping="Wrap"
        VerticalAlignment="Top" Width="120"/>
        <TextBlock HorizontalAlignment="Left"
        Margin="282,96,0,0" TextWrapping="Wrap" Text="A =
        (a + b) / 2 * h" VerticalAlignment="Top" Height="32"
        Width="150"/>
        <TextBox x:Name="b_input" HorizontalAlignment="Left"
        Height="23" Margin="226,187,0,0" TextWrapping="Wrap"
        VerticalAlignment="Top" Width="120"/>
        <TextBox x:Name="h_input" HorizontalAlignment="Left"
        Height="23" Margin="545,187,0,0" TextWrapping="Wrap"
        VerticalAlignment="Top" Width="120"/>
        <TextBlock HorizontalAlignment="Left"
        Margin="118,187,0,0" TextWrapping="Wrap" Text="A="
        VerticalAlignment="Top" Height="23" Width="28"/>
        <TextBlock  x:Name="A_output"
        HorizontalAlignment="Left" Margin="151,187,0,0"
        TextWrapping="Wrap" VerticalAlignment="Top" Height="23"
        Width="28"/>
        <Button  Click="Button_Click" Content="Calculate"
        HorizontalAlignment="Left" Margin="10,187,0,0"
        VerticalAlignment="Top" Width="75"/>
</Grid>
```

Finally, for the trapezoid calculator, we have all the same things in the XAML (see Figure 1-18, Listing 1-20) – text blocks, text boxes for input, and a button to execute calculation.

Listing 1-21. Button click event for calculation

```
private void Button_Click(object sender, RoutedEventArgs e)
        {
            try
            {
                A_output.Text =( (Convert.ToDouble(a_input.
                Text) + Convert.ToDouble(b_input.Text)) / 2 *
                Convert.ToDouble(h_input.Text)).ToString();
            }
            catch (Exception ex)
            {
                A_output.Text = "N/A";
            }
        }
```

The C# part here (See Listing 1-21) is a bit more complex, but the idea is still the same – we make the calculation, convert the result to string, and set it to Text property.

Throughout this project, you may have noticed a certain naming system for the elements. For the inputs, we have letter in formula followed by an underscore and then followed by the word input. Then, we have formula letter followed by an underscore and then followed by the word output for the TextBlock output. Naming systems are very important in XAML, as some views may contain a lot more elements than you have seen here. It can also make your life easier when you are typing the name of the element in the C# code.

Now you know how to use some basic common events and access some UI elements. In the next chapter, we will explore some more events, the kind that can be applied to the window or application wide. Then in the third chapter, we will be able to look at some more UI elements that will be very useful in your projects.

CHAPTER 2

Events

Everything in WPF is based on events, like the click and change events, and although most of them are associated with specific elements, there are some that are more generic. In this chapter, you will learn how to use window-wide, application-wide, and other kinds of generic events.

Application Events

The application events and anything that is general about the whole application will be found in App.xaml.cs file. You will see why the XAML part of it exists in Chapter 6 of this book.

Listing 2-1. App.xaml.cs contents

```
public partial class App : Application
    {
        protected override void OnActivated(EventArgs e)
        {
            base.OnActivated(e);
        }

        protected override void OnDeactivated(EventArgs e)
        {
            base.OnDeactivated(e);
        }
```

```
protected override void OnExit(ExitEventArgs e)
{
    base.OnExit(e);
}

protected override void OnStartup(StartupEventArgs e)
{
    base.OnStartup(e);
}
}
```

There are four events to look (See Listing 2-1) at in terms of the application. You will see that some of these will be identical to the ones found in a window, but these are application-wide events, and those will be only in the window scope.

First, we have OnActivated and OnDeactivated; these will occur basically whenever one of your windows gains or loses focus. Now, if the user uses your application and then goes into their browser, your application will lose focus and OnDeactived will occur. And then once the user comes back to your application, OnActivated will occur. You must be extremely careful with these events as they may cause your application to enter a continuous loop in some arrangements.

We also have OnExit, which occurs when application closes, but it does not have a way to prevent it closing. That will be done in a Window. The other one is quite the opposite, OnStartup, which occurs when the application starts.

Mouse Events

In general, you do not really need to handle mouse events in WPF; instead, you have button click, text box focused, and others. But sometimes, mouse

events might be quite useful for games, drawing tools, and many other
occasions. We will first look at basic events that a mouse can have, and
then you will learn how to deal with coordinates.

Listing 2-2. Events for the window

```
public MainWindow()
        {
            InitializeComponent();
            //MouseDoubleClick += MainWindow_MouseDoubleClick;
           MouseRightButtonDown += MainWindow_
           MouseRightButtonDown;
            MouseLeftButtonDown += MainWindow_
            MouseLeftButtonDown;

        }

        private void MainWindow_MouseLeftButtonDown(object
        sender, MouseButtonEventArgs e)
        {
            MessageBox.Show("left click");
        }

        private void MainWindow_MouseRightButtonDown(object
        sender, MouseButtonEventArgs e)
        {
            MessageBox.Show("right click");
        }

        private void MainWindow_MouseDoubleClick(object sender,
        MouseButtonEventArgs e)
        {
```

```
    if (e.LeftButton == MouseButtonState.Pressed)
    {
        MessageBox.Show("double click - left");
    }

    if (e.RightButton == MouseButtonState.Pressed)
    {
        MessageBox.Show("double click - right");
    }

}
```

First of all, you need to know three main events for the mouse (See Listing 2-2). The MouseDoubleClick event will occur when the user double-clicks either the left or the right mouse button, the MouseRightButtonDown event will occur when the user clicks the right mouse button, and the MouseLeftButtonDown event will occur when the user clicks the left mouse button. Another important thing is getting the state of the button which had the event. To do that, you need to access the MouseButtonEventArgs event where you will find states for the left, right, and middle mouse buttons. You will see why this is useful in the "Quick Example" section of this chapter. The final thing to understand in this example is the commented out MouseDoubleClick; there would be no problem if this was left uncommented, but to actually test this feature, you would need to comment or remove the other events because they interfere with each other.

Listing 2-3. Example grid with text block inside

```
<Grid x:Name="grd1" Background="Transparent">
    <TextBlock x:Name="tb1" HorizontalAlignment="Left"
    Margin="353,100,0,0" TextWrapping="Wrap"
    VerticalAlignment="Top" Width="55"/>
</Grid>
```

36

To get the current position of the mouse, you need to have an area of relativity. In this case, that will be the grid, and with that, we have a text box in which the coordinates will be displayed.

Listing 2-4. Mouse events for the example

```
public MainWindow()
        {
            InitializeComponent();
            grd1.MouseDown += Grd1_MouseDown;
            //grd1.MouseEnter += Grd1_MouseEnter;
            grd1.MouseMove += Grd1_MouseMove;
            grd1.MouseLeave += Grd1_MouseLeave;
        }

        private void Grd1_MouseMove(object sender,
        MouseEventArgs e)
        {
            tb1.Text = e.GetPosition(grd1).X.ToString() + ":" +
            e.GetPosition(grd1).Y.ToString();
        }

        private void Grd1_MouseLeave(object sender,
        MouseEventArgs e)
        {
            tb1.Text = "Mouse left";
        }

        private void Grd1_MouseEnter(object sender,
        MouseEventArgs e)
        {
            MessageBox.Show(e.GetPosition(grd1).X.ToString() +
            ":" + e.GetPosition(grd1).Y.ToString());
        }
```

```
private void Grd1_MouseDown(object sender,
MouseButtonEventArgs e)
{
    MessageBox.Show(e.GetPosition(grd1).X.ToString() +
    ":" + e.GetPosition(grd1).Y.ToString());
}
```

For the mouse movements, we have several different events (See Listing 2-4) – MouseEnter which occurs when the mouse enters the relative area, MouseMove which occurs whenever the mouse moves in the relative area (in this case, the grid), and MouseLeave which occurs when the mouse leaves the area. One thing to note here is the commented out MouseEnter event; in this example, on MouseEnter, we display a message box, which essentially makes the cursor leave the grid (relative area), and so once the user dismisses the message box, the mouse will enter again and the message box will pop up again, which essentially breaks the program.

Keyboard Events

When it comes to keyboard events, you only need to know two events related to keyboard. The most difficult part is retrieving the pressed key value.

Listing 2-5. Keyboard events

```
public MainWindow()
    {
        InitializeComponent();
        KeyDown += MainWindow_KeyDown;
        KeyUp += MainWindow_KeyUp;
    }
```

```
private void MainWindow_KeyUp(object sender,
KeyEventArgs e)
{
    MessageBox.Show(e.Key.ToString());
}

private void MainWindow_KeyDown(object sender,
KeyEventArgs e)
{
    if (e.Key == Key.Enter)
    {
        MessageBox.Show(e.Key.ToString());
    }
}
```

The example here (See Listing 2-5) is quite straightforward – you do not need any additional XAML code to handle keyboard event (or key) events. The first event is KeyDown – this will occur when you press the key; the next one is KeyUp – this one will only occur after you release the pressed key. To retrieve a value for the key, you need to access the KeyEventArgs and Key property in it. The Key property is actually an enumerable, so you do not need to compare it as a string, which is helpful with the more exotic keys.

Window Events

There are basically four main window events, and most of them do not have any features. These can be very useful on certain occasions, but it can also be tricky to use them and you have to be extra careful.

Listing 2-6. Window events

```
protected override void OnClosing(CancelEventArgs e)
        {
            if (MessageBox.Show("Are you sure you want
            to leave?","",MessageBoxButton.YesNo) ==
            MessageBoxResult.No)
            {
                e.Cancel = true;
            }
            base.OnClosing(e);
        }

        protected override void OnClosed(EventArgs e)
        {
            base.OnClosed(e);
        }

        protected override void OnActivated(EventArgs e)
        {
            base.OnActivated(e);
        }

        protected override void OnDeactivated(EventArgs e)
        {
            base.OnActivated(e);
        }

        protected override void OnInitialized(EventArgs e)
        {
            base.OnInitialized(e);
        }
```

The first event, (See Listing 2-6), OnClosing, is probably the most exciting one. It will occur when the user attempts to close the window (not after it is closed). This event has CancelEventArgs, and you only really care about the Cancel property. As you can see in the example, we have a message box which asks the user if they really want to leave, and if they decide not to leave, the program sets the Cancel property to false. When it is set to false, the window will not be closed. However, you have to be careful and not overcomplicate such arrangement, as failure would mean that the user has to close the program from task manager, which is really bad.

After OnClosing (unless Cancel is set to true), another event will occur – OnClosed. This one does not have any specific features, but it can be useful to save some data, create backup save file, disconnect connections, or clear some data.

The next two events are OnActivated and OnDeactivated; these are very similar and opposite. The OnActivated occurs basically when the window gets focused, and the OnDeactivated occurs when the window loses focus. So, it is not about opening or closing the window. This is useful when you have several windows in your arrangement and you want to save resources when something does not need to be displayed.

Finally, we have OnInitialized, which occurs when the window is opened. You can execute code here instead of doing it in window constructor after the InitalizeComponent method.

Quick Example

In this example, you will see how you can create a simple drag and drop arrangement using only the mouse events.

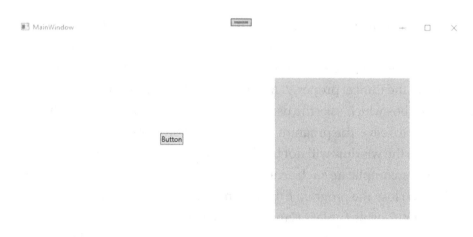

Figure 2-1. Initial view of the example

Initially, we have a button and a gray grid – the button is outside of the grid.

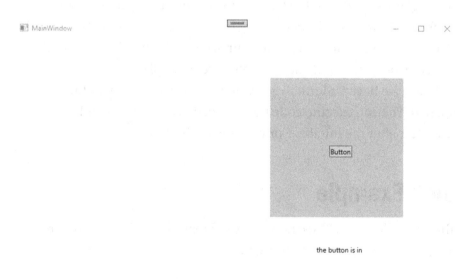

Figure 2-2. Button dragged onto the grid

Once the button is dragged onto the grid, the text will be displayed saying "the button is in" (Compare Figure 2-1 and Figure 2-2).

Listing 2-7. Grid layout for the example

```
<Grid x:Name="grd" MouseMove="Grid_MouseMove">
        <Grid Margin="450,70,100,100" Background="LightGray"/>
        <Button x:Name="bt1" Content="Button"
        HorizontalAlignment="Left" Margin="251,165,0,0"
        VerticalAlignment="Top"/>
        <Label x:Name="lb" HorizontalAlignment="Left"
        Margin="526,354,0,0" VerticalAlignment="Top"
        Width="92"/>
</Grid>
```

In the main grid, we have another grid with a gray background color set. We also have a button, which will be dragged, and a label to display the text. You may also notice that the main Grid has a name and a MouseMove event relative to it (See Listing 2-7). Also, since we want to drag the button onto the grid, in the XAML code, the button element needs to go below the grid (that way, it is on top).

Listing 2-8. Mouse event for the example

```
private void Grid_MouseMove(object sender, MouseEventArgs e)
        {
            if (bt1.IsMouseOver && e.RightButton ==
            MouseButtonState.Pressed)
            {
                    bt1.Margin = new Thickness(e.
                    GetPosition(grd).X - 25,
                    e.GetPosition(grd).Y - 10, 0, 0);
```

```
if (e.GetPosition(grd).X - 25 < 700
&& e.GetPosition(grd).X - 25 > 450
&& e.GetPosition(grd).Y - 10 > 70 &&
e.GetPosition(grd).Y - 10 < 300)
{
    lb.Content = "the button is in the grid";
}
    }
}
```

In the C# code (See Listing 2-8), we only have one event, the MouseMove event. Remember, the MouseMove event occurs whenever the mouse moves on every pixel, so with that, we need to have some logic inside the event method. Since we drag the button, we need to check for the mouse to be over the button; that is why we use IsMouseOver. We also check for the right button to be clicked; only if that is the case, it will be dragged.

The position is set on every movement, but to make this work properly, we need to have a little buffer on each side. If you set the current position of the mouse directly, your cursor will always be on the corner, and it will be difficult to use. Finally, we have an if statement which checks that the button is in the grid according to the margin values of the grid.

Quick Exercise

For this exercise, your task is to establish the user details form on the main window. The form will contain two inputs – full name and user bio. If the user hovers on the name input box, under it, a text should be displayed saying "Enter your full name", and if the user hovers on the bio input box, the text displayed will be "This is description about you". Finally, the user should receive notice if they try to exit when any of the text boxes have some text in them.

You may use the Visible property to handle visibility of elements in WPF.

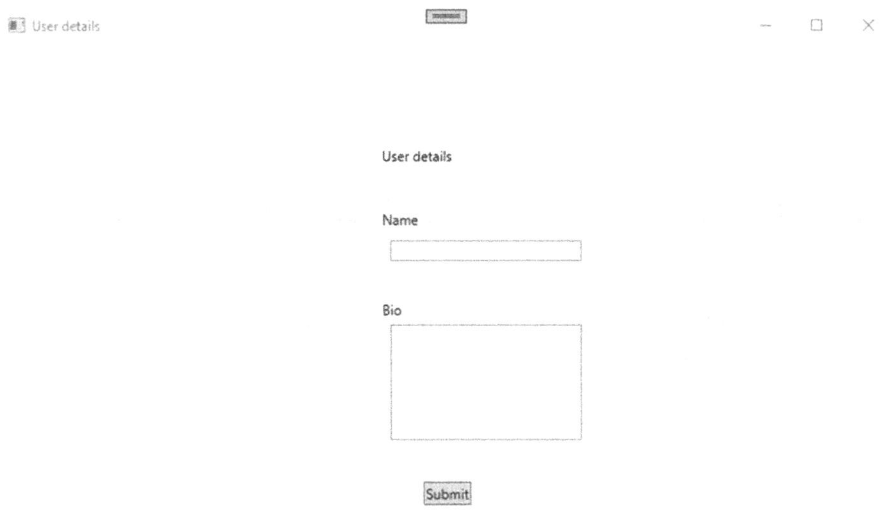
User details
User details
Name
Bio
Submit

Figure 2-3. *Initial view of the example*

Initially, the layout is quite simple, displaying the window with the new title, couple of input boxes, and a submit button.

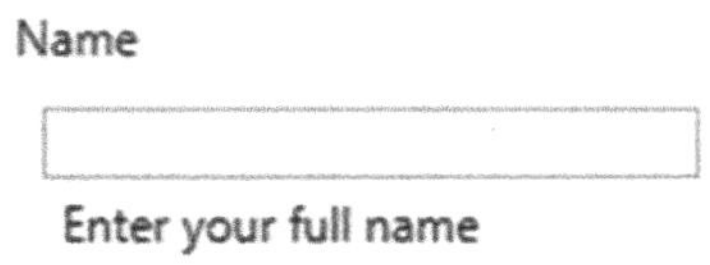
Name
Enter your full name

Figure 2-4. *Text box description after the user hovers on the text box*

Figure 2-5. *Text box description after the user hovers over the text box*

Once the user hovers one of the input boxes (See Figure 2-4, Figure 2-5), the description for them will be displayed.

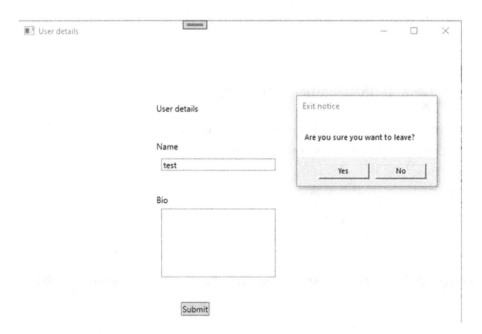

Figure 2-6.

Finally, if any of the text boxes have some text inside them, the system will ask the user if they really want to leave and lose the data.

Listing 2-9. Window for the example

```
<Window x:Class="WpfApp1.MainWindow"
        xmlns="http://schemas.microsoft.com/winfx/2006/xaml/
        presentation"
        xmlns:x="http://schemas.microsoft.com/winfx/2006/xaml"
        xmlns:d="http://schemas.microsoft.com/expression/
        blend/2008"
        xmlns:mc="http://schemas.openxmlformats.org/markup-
        compatibility/2006"
        xmlns:local="clr-namespace:WpfApp1"
        mc:Ignorable="d"
        Title="User details" Height="450" Width="800">
    <Grid>
        <Label Content="User details"
        HorizontalAlignment="Center" Margin="0,84,0,0"
        VerticalAlignment="Top" Width="124"/>
        <Label Content="Name" HorizontalAlignment="Center"
        Margin="0,139,0,0" VerticalAlignment="Top" Width="124"/>
        <Label Content="Bio" HorizontalAlignment="Center"
        Margin="0,217,0,0" VerticalAlignment="Top" Width="124"/>
        <TextBox  MouseEnter="namebox_MouseEnter"
        MouseLeave="namebox_MouseLeave" x:Name="namebox"
        HorizontalAlignment="Left" Margin="342,170,0,0"
        TextWrapping="Wrap" VerticalAlignment="Top"
        Width="168"/>
```

```
<TextBox  MouseEnter="biobox_MouseEnter"
MouseLeave="biobox_MouseLeave" x:Name="biobox"
HorizontalAlignment="Left" Margin="342,243,0,0"
TextWrapping="Wrap" VerticalAlignment="Top" Width="168"
Height="100"/>
<Button Content="Submit" HorizontalAlignment="Center"
Margin="0,379,0,0" VerticalAlignment="Top"/>
<Label Visibility="Collapsed" x:Name="labelalert2"
Content="This is description about you"
HorizontalAlignment="Left" Margin="342,343,0,0"
VerticalAlignment="Top" Width="168" Height="31"/>
<Label Visibility="Collapsed" x:Name="labelalert1"
Content="Enter your full name"
HorizontalAlignment="Left" Margin="342,186,0,0"
VerticalAlignment="Top" Width="168" Height="31"/>
    </Grid>
</Window>
```

From the XAML perspective, everything is quite basic (See Listing 2-9). But you do have to pay special attention here to the labels, used to display description about the text boxes. Since we only want to display these when the user hovers on text boxes, you have to set some initial values. It can be done in the window constructor, but it is more appropriate and easier to read if they are set in the XAML. You should also notice the Title property for the window set to "User details".

Listing 2-10. Window contents for C# code

```
protected override void OnClosing(CancelEventArgs e)
        {
            if (namebox.Text.Length > 0 || biobox.Text.Length > 0)
            {
```

```
    if (MessageBox.Show("Are you sure you want to
    leave?","Exit notice",MessageBoxButton.YesNo) ==
    MessageBoxResult.No)
    {
        e.Cancel = true;
    }
}
base.OnClosing(e);
}

private void namebox_MouseEnter(object sender,
MouseEventArgs e)
{
    labelalert1.Visibility = Visibility.Visible;
}

private void namebox_MouseLeave(object sender,
MouseEventArgs e)
{
    labelalert1.Visibility = Visibility.Collapsed;
}

private void biobox_MouseEnter(object sender,
MouseEventArgs e)
{
    labelalert2.Visibility = Visibility.Visible;
}

private void biobox_MouseLeave(object sender,
MouseEventArgs e)
{
    labelalert2.Visibility = Visibility.Collapsed;
}
```

After the XAML, we have some events in C# (See Listing 2-10). First, you may see the MouseEnter and MouseLeave events for both namebox and biobox. On the MouseEnter event, we set visibility to Visible, and on the MouseLeave event, we set Collapsed. Now, in your attempt on this exercise, you may have used Hidden instead of Collapsed, and it would be fine as well. Finally, we have an OnClosing event for the window. In it, we check for the text boxes to have some characters inserted; if they are empty, the window will be closed. If they do contain something, we display a message box, and if the answer is No, we cancel the closing of the window.

CHAPTER 3

UI Elements

So far, you have seen a handful of elements; you have also seen some events and how they function. But now, it is time to get familiar with several more of the most common WPF UI elements. You will learn how to deal with lists and how to draw on canvas and deal with many other elements.

Progress Bar

Progress bar is one of the more important elements of WPF; it may not seem that way, but it is always better to display when something is loading so that no more action would be taken as that may lead to crashes. There are two ways that it can work – it can increase incrementally, or you can make it indeterminate. With that, you can change colors and make some other simple design changes to fit your theme.

Listing 3-1. XAML code for MainWindow.xaml

```
<Grid>
        <ProgressBar x:Name="pbar" HorizontalAlignment="Left"
        Height="14" Margin="155,95,0,0" VerticalAlignment="Top"
        Width="570"/>
        <Button Click="Button_Click" Content="step1"
        HorizontalAlignment="Left" Margin="155,146,0,0"
        VerticalAlignment="Top" Width="97">
```

© Taurius Litvinavicius 2021
T. Litvinavicius, *Exploring Windows Presentation Foundation*,
https://doi.org/10.1007/978-1-4842-6637-3_3

```
</Button>
<Button Click="Button_Click_1" Content="step2"
HorizontalAlignment="Left" Margin="284,146,0,0"
VerticalAlignment="Top" Width="75"/>
<Button Click="Button_Click_2" Content="step3"
HorizontalAlignment="Left" Margin="500,146,0,0"
VerticalAlignment="Top" Width="75"/>
<Button Click="Button_Click_3" Content="step4"
HorizontalAlignment="Left" Margin="628,146,0,0"
VerticalAlignment="Top" Width="75"/>
<Button Click="Button_Click_4" Content="start"
HorizontalAlignment="Left" Margin="392,195,0,0"
VerticalAlignment="Top" Width="75"/>
```

```
</Grid>
```

The example shows how you can increase the bar incrementally and how it can be made indefinite. The progress bar itself is named pbar. With it, you can find several buttons (See Listing 3-1); the first four buttons will increase the bar by 25%, and the last one will make it indeterminate.

Listing 3-2. C# code in MainWindow.xaml.cs

```
private void Button_Click(object sender, RoutedEventArgs e)
        {
            pbar.Value += 25;
        }

        private void Button_Click_1(object sender,
        RoutedEventArgs e)
        {
            pbar.Value += 25;

        }
```

```
private void Button_Click_2(object sender,
RoutedEventArgs e)
{
    pbar.Value += 25;
}

private void Button_Click_3(object sender,
RoutedEventArgs e)
{
    pbar.Value += 25;
}

private void Button_Click_4(object sender,
RoutedEventArgs e)
{
    pbar.IsIndeterminate = true;
}
```

The bar has a property called Value, which basically determines how much of the background is filled. The value goes from 1 to 100, but it is a double type; therefore, the increments can be quite small.

Figure 3-1. *Progress bar after "step1" increase*

When the "step1" button is clicked (See Listing 3-2), the Value property is set to 25 (see Figure 3-1); hence, you can see the progress bar filled 25%. The progress bar also has an IsIndeterminate property, which if set to true will make the progress bar run indeterminately; to stop it, simply set the property to false.

53

For the design (See Listing 3-1), you can change the size and orientation in the XAML editor; besides that, you might also want to change the color.

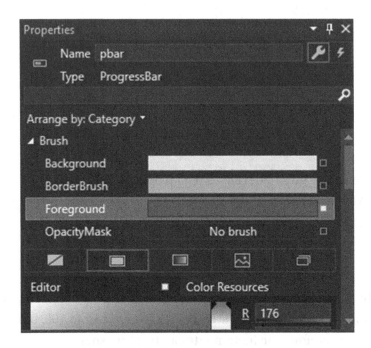

Figure 3-2. *Progress bar properties in XAML designer*

To do that, simply select the progress bar, go to the properties (see Figure 3-2), and find Foreground in the Brush section.

Listing 3-3. Foreground property set in C#

```
pbar.Foreground = new SolidColorBrush(Color.FromRgb(56, 20, 122));
```

To set this or any other color property in C#, you need to use SolidColorBrush type and in it provide Color.FromRgb return value (See Listing 3-3).

Tabs

In the first chapter, you saw two main ways of arranging the elements – window and page. Tabs is another option you may use, although it is a bit different and it will not have separate code-behind files for each view.

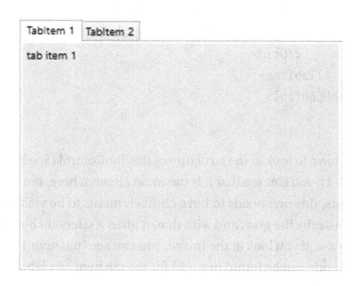

Figure 3-3. *Tab view*

In this example, everything will be done in XAML. You can see (Figure 3-3) that we have two tab items (or two buttons for them). Basically, if you click one of the buttons, a view will open for that specific tab. In a way, these are always opened – they do not refresh when you open another one.

Listing 3-4. XAML code for MainWindow.xaml

```
<Grid>
        <TabControl HorizontalAlignment="Left" Height="266"
        Margin="10,87,0,0" VerticalAlignment="Top" Width="346">
```

```
            <TabItem  Header="TabItem 1">
                <Grid Background="#FFE5E5E5">
                    <Label>tab item 1</Label>
                </Grid>
            </TabItem>
            <TabItem Header="TabItem 2">
                <Grid Background="#FFE5E5E5">
                    <Label>tab item 2</Label>
                </Grid>
            </TabItem>
        </TabControl>

</Grid>
```

First, we have to look at the structure of the TabControl (See Figure 3-3 and Listing 3-4); you can see that it is the main element here, but unlike most elements, this one needs to have child elements to be viable. TabItem is basically the gray, and with that, it gives a selection button (on top). In this case, if you look at the image, you can see "tab item 1" display, which in the code can be found in a grid for the tab item as a label. The header value is displayed for the button. Other than that, you can change colors for grids and the buttons themselves (TabItem) and do other design changes, but you do not need to do anything in the C# code.

Radio Button

Radio button and check box may seem very similar, but actually the use cases are quite different. The main feature of a radio button is to be in a group, and in a group, only one radio button can be selected.

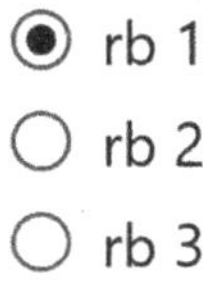

◉ rb 1
○ rb 2
○ rb 3

Figure 3-4. *Group of radio buttons*

Listing 3-5. XAML code for MainWindow.xaml

```
<Grid>
        <RadioButton x:Name="rb1"    IsChecked="True"
        GroupName="gr1" Content="rb 1"
        HorizontalAlignment="Left" Margin="342,130,0,0"
        VerticalAlignment="Top"/>
        <RadioButton x:Name="rb3"    GroupName="gr1"
        Content="rb 3" HorizontalAlignment="Left"
        Margin="342,170,0,0" VerticalAlignment="Top"/>
        <RadioButton x:Name="rb2"    GroupName="gr1"
        Content="rb 2" HorizontalAlignment="Left"
        Margin="342,150,0,0" VerticalAlignment="Top"/>
</Grid>
```

You can see here (Figure 3-4) the radio buttons are defined in XAML, and there is something very important set on each one of them. That is the GroupName property, and all the buttons named with the same name will be in the same group. In other words, only one of those buttons will be selected at any given time. We also have IsChecked set to true for the first one; it is important to set at least one value like that; otherwise, you might have issues with form submissions or similar arrangements.

Listing 3-6. Event for radio buttons

```
public MainWindow()
        {
            InitializeComponent();
            rb1.Checked += RadioButton_Checked;
            rb2.Checked += RadioButton_Checked_1;
            rb3.Checked += RadioButton_Checked_2;
        }

        private void RadioButton_Checked(object sender,
        RoutedEventArgs e)
        {
            MessageBox.Show("1");
            if ((bool)rb1.IsChecked)
            {
                MessageBox.Show("1 is checked");
            }
        }

        private void RadioButton_Checked_1(object sender,
        RoutedEventArgs e)
        {
            MessageBox.Show("2");
        }

        private void RadioButton_Checked_2(object sender,
        RoutedEventArgs e)
        {
            MessageBox.Show("3");
        }
```

The Checked event (See Listing 3-6) occurs whenever a specific check box is checked (See Figure 3-4).

Check Box

A check box is one of the more common elements in WPF, and it is quite straightforward to use. You have a Boolean value and then some text to describe it.

Figure 3-5. *Check box arrangement*

Listing 3-7. XAML code for the check box example

```
<Grid>
        <CheckBox Checked="Cb1_Checked" Unchecked="cb1_
        Unchecked" x:Name="cb1" Content="box 1"
        HorizontalAlignment="Left" Margin="224,115,0,0"
        VerticalAlignment="Top" Width="97"/>
        <CheckBox Checked="Cb2_Checked" Unchecked="cb2_
        Unchecked" x:Name="cb2" Content="box 2"
        HorizontalAlignment="Left" Margin="338,115,0,0"
        VerticalAlignment="Top" Width="97"/>
        <CheckBox Checked="Cb3_Checked" Unchecked="cb3_
        Unchecked" x:Name="cb3" Content="box 3"
        HorizontalAlignment="Left" Margin="453,115,0,0"
        VerticalAlignment="Top" Width="97"/>
        <TextBlock HorizontalAlignment="Left"
        Margin="285,67,0,0" TextWrapping="Wrap" Text="display:
        " VerticalAlignment="Top" Width="55"/>
```

```
<TextBlock x:Name="tb1" HorizontalAlignment="Left"
Margin="345,67,0,0" TextWrapping="Wrap"
VerticalAlignment="Top" Width="48"/>
</Grid>
```

In this example (see Figure 3-5), we have three check boxes and one text block to display some text (See Listing 3-7). The check boxes go from 1 to 3, and if one of them is checked, the number of it will be displayed. Check boxes have two main events – Checked and Unchecked; one occurs when the box gets checked and then the other when it gets unchecked.

Listing 3-8. XAML code for check box events and example

```
void createdisplay()
    {
        tb1.Text = "";
        string displaystring = "";
        if (cb1.IsChecked == true)
        {
            displaystring += "1 ";
        }
        if (cb2.IsChecked == true)
        {
            displaystring += "2 ";
        }
        if (cb3.IsChecked == true)
        {
            displaystring += "3 ";
        }

        tb1.Text = displaystring.ToString();
    }
```

```
private void Cb1_Checked(object sender, RoutedEventArgs e)
{
    createdisplay();
}

private void Cb2_Checked(object sender, RoutedEventArgs e)
{
    createdisplay();
}

private void Cb3_Checked(object sender, RoutedEventArgs e)
{
    createdisplay();
}

private void cb1_Unchecked(object sender,
RoutedEventArgs e)
{
    createdisplay();
}

private void cb2_Unchecked(object sender,
RoutedEventArgs e)
{
    createdisplay();
}

private void cb3_Unchecked(object sender,
RoutedEventArgs e)
{
    createdisplay();
}
```

In this example (See Figure 3-5), we go for a more direct option; we have a method createdisplay() (See Listing 3-5) which uses if statements to see whether a specific box is checked or unchecked and displays specific value accordingly. To look up the status of the box, you need to access the IsChecked property. Alternatively, the sender object in the events would be of type CheckBox (for that specific check box), and you could look up the values from there.

Slider

A slider is good when you need the user to choose a value in a predefined range and display calculations as they change the value. In general, it is simple to use, but there are some things that you have to be careful of.

Figure 3-6. *Slider showcase*

Listing 3-9. XAML code for the slider showcase

```
<Grid>
        <Slider ValueChanged="Sld_ValueChanged"
        Maximum="1000"  x:Name="sld" HorizontalAlignment="Left"
        Margin="280,128,0,0" VerticalAlignment="Top"
        Width="288"/>
        <TextBlock x:Name="tb1" HorizontalAlignment="Left"
        Margin="388,90,0,0" TextWrapping="Wrap"
        VerticalAlignment="Top" Width="68"/>
</Grid>
```

As you can see (Figure 3-6), in this example, we have a slider and a text block, where we display the value of the slider (See Listing 3-9). The tricky part with the slider is that you can set some properties in XAML, but if you set some of them in XAML, the program will fail.

Listing 3-10. C# code for the showcase

```
public MainWindow()
        {
            InitializeComponent();
            sld.Minimum = 100;
            sld.Value = 200;
        }

        private void Sld_ValueChanged(object sender,
        RoutedPropertyChangedEventArgs<double> e)
        {
                tb1.Text = e.NewValue.ToString();
        }
```

As you can see in the example (See Figure 3-6), you can set the Maximum property, but for the Minimum property, you have to set it in the C# code (See Listing 3-10). The value should also be set in the C# code. Other than that, you simply need to use ValueChanged event, and from there, you will retrieve the current value by accessing the RoutedPropertyChangedEventArgs NewValue property.

Image

Listing 3-11. XAML code for the example

```
<Grid>
        <Image x:Name="img1" HorizontalAlignment="Left"
        Height="268" Margin="140,70,0,0"
        VerticalAlignment="Top" Width="534"  />
        <Button Content="show" HorizontalAlignment="Left"
        Margin="338,361,0,0" VerticalAlignment="Top" Width="74"
        Click="Button_Click"/>
</Grid>
```

In this example (See Listing 3-11), we have our Image element, which has a name and a pre-set size. With it, there is a button which when clicked will retrieve and display an image.

Listing 3-12. C# code for the example button click event

```
private void Button_Click(object sender, RoutedEventArgs e)
        {
            FileStream flstr = new FileStream("D:\\test\\test1.
            png", FileMode.Open);
            var imgsrc = new BitmapImage();
            imgsrc.BeginInit();
            imgsrc.StreamSource = flstr;
            imgsrc.EndInit();
            img1.Source = imgsrc;
        }
```

To set the source, you first need to establish a file stream (See Listing 3-12). Then you need to create and initialize the BitmapImage, then set source (the FileStream), and then stop the initialization using the EndInit method. Finally, you set the BitmapImage as your Source for Image element. In case you want to set it as from url, you can use UriSource instead of StreamSource.

Media Element

The Media element in WPF can also be referred to as video player, as that is what it does. It will take a file, it will read it, and it will display the video. You also have controls and many other options.

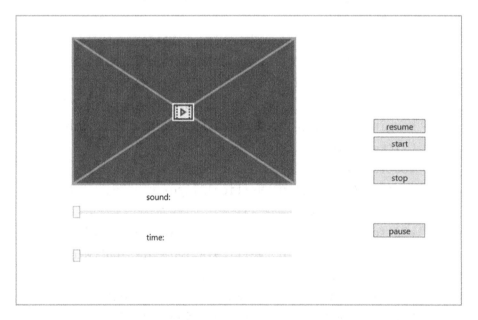

Figure 3-7. *Media element and other elements in XAML design view*

In the XAML editor (see Figure 3-7), we have the media element placed in the middle; below it, we have two sliders – one for sound volume and the other for adjusting time of the video. We also have four buttons: the start button will load the video file and start playing it, the pause button

65

will simply pause the video, the resume button will resume the video from the same spot, and the stop button will stop the video, and if you resume it after that, it will start from the beginning.

Listing 3-13. XAML code for the example

```
<Grid>
        <MediaElement LoadedBehavior="Manual"
        UnloadedBehavior="Manual" x:Name="md"
        HorizontalAlignment="Left" Height="211"
        Margin="222,33,0,0" VerticalAlignment="Top"
        Width="326"/>
        <Button Content="start" HorizontalAlignment="Left"
        Margin="664,175,0,0" VerticalAlignment="Top" Width="75"
        Click="Button_Click"/>
        <Button Content="stop" HorizontalAlignment="Left"
        Margin="664,224,0,0" VerticalAlignment="Top" Width="75"
        Click="Button_Click_1"/>
        <Button Content="pause" HorizontalAlignment="Left"
        Margin="664,301,0,0" VerticalAlignment="Top" Width="75"
        Click="Button_Click_2"/>
        <Button Content="resume" HorizontalAlignment="Left"
        Margin="664,150,0,0" VerticalAlignment="Top" Width="75"
        Click="Button_Click_3"/>
        <Label Content="sound:" HorizontalAlignment="Left"
        Margin="326,249,0,0" VerticalAlignment="Top"
        Width="53"/>
        <Label x:Name="soundlabel" Content=""
        HorizontalAlignment="Left" Margin="379,249,0,0"
        VerticalAlignment="Top" Width="41"/>
```

```
<Slider x:Name="soundslider" ValueChanged="Soundslider_
ValueChanged" HorizontalAlignment="Left"
Margin="222,275,0,0" VerticalAlignment="Top"
Width="326"/>
<Slider x:Name="timeslider" ValueChanged="Timeslider_
ValueChanged" HorizontalAlignment="Left"
Margin="222,338,0,0" VerticalAlignment="Top"
Width="326"/>
<Label Content="time: " HorizontalAlignment="Left"
Margin="326,307,0,0" VerticalAlignment="Top"
Width="53"/>
<Label x:Name="timelabel" Content=""
HorizontalAlignment="Left" Margin="379,307,0,0"
VerticalAlignment="Top" Width="41"/>
```
</Grid>

The media element has two properties, and those are very important (See Listing 3-13). You should always set LoadedBehavior and UnloadedBehavior to Manual; this way, you can control everything yourself. Every other element simply has either a name, an event, or both (See Figure 3-7).

Listing 3-14. "start" button click event

```
private void Button_Click(object sender, RoutedEventArgs e)
        {
                md.Source = new System.Uri("D:\\test\\testfile.
                mp4");

                md.Play();

                while (md.NaturalDuration.HasTimeSpan == false)
                { }
```

```
            timeslider.Maximum = md.NaturalDuration.
            TimeSpan.TotalSeconds;
            soundslider.Maximum = 1;
    }
```

This event (See Listing 3-14) is for the start button, and before anything else, you can see that the source is set as Uri. After that, we need to use the Play method to start playing the file. We also have a while loop, an empty one, which may seem rather strange, but there is a good reason for it. The time span will take some time to load after the play was initiated, but we need to set the timeslider maximum at some point. This is the total amount in seconds for the video, the slider will set new value for the media element, and that is how it will move, but if you set it too large, it will break. We also set soundslider to 1, because the volume is from 0 to 1.

Listing 3-15. Button events for video controls

```
private void Button_Click_1(object sender, RoutedEventArgs e)
    {
        md.Stop();
    }

    private void Button_Click_2(object sender,
    RoutedEventArgs e)
    {
        md.Pause();
    }

    private void Button_Click_3(object sender,
    RoutedEventArgs e)
    {
        md.Play();
    }
```

After the initial load, we have three more events (See Listing 3-15) and with that three more methods. The Stop method will completely stop it and basically get back to the beginning. The Pause method will also stop the video, but it will stay at the current point, and then the Play method will start playing again at whatever position the video is.

Listing 3-16. Soundslider ValueChanged event

```
private void Soundslider_ValueChanged(object sender,
RoutedPropertyChangedEventArgs<double> e)
        {
            md.Volume = e.NewValue;
        }
```

The slider's ValueChanged event simply sets the Volume property of the media element (See Listing 3-16). Since it was previously set as maximum 1, the value set will be between 0 and 1.

Listing 3-17. timeslider ValueChanged event

```
private void Timeslider_ValueChanged(object sender,
RoutedPropertyChangedEventArgs<double> e)
        {
            md.Pause();
            md.Position = new TimeSpan(0,0,Convert.
            ToInt32(Math.Round(e.NewValue)));
            timelabel.Content = md.Position.TotalSeconds;
            md.Play();
        }
```

The time change is a bit more complex than the sound volume. What we want to set is Position (See Listing 3-17), but since the Position is always changing, we first need to stop the video. Now, the slider is only one number, seconds, but the Position is TimeSpan. So, you need to pause the video to keep the Position stationary, then set the Position, and then play again.

Menu

A menu item is basically a way to arrange several buttons and have expandable lists of buttons. Although a very simple element, it can be extremely useful, and almost every program uses it to some extent.

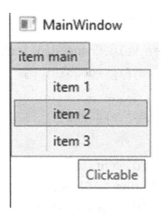

Figure 3-8. *Menu display*

Listing 3-18. XAML code for Menu example

```
<Grid>
        <Menu HorizontalAlignment="Left" Height="24"
        VerticalAlignment="Top" Width="792">
            <MenuItem Header="item main" Height="24"
            Width="71">
                <MenuItem Header="item 1"  Height="24"
                Width="120"/>
                <MenuItem Click="MenuItem_Click" Header="item
                2" Height="24" Width="120">
                    <MenuItem.ToolTip>
                        Clickable
                    </MenuItem.ToolTip>
                </MenuItem>
```

```
            <MenuItem Header="item 3" Height="24"
            Width="120"/>
        </MenuItem>
    </Menu>
</Grid>
```

This item (see Listing 3-18) is quite complex in its structure, but it does not really have any C# functionality. The main element is menu, and in that, you can have MenuItem elements (see Figure 3-8), and those can contain more MenuItem elements.

List View

List view is a bit more complicated than most of the other elements covered here. It is a very useful element, but setting values and then retrieving them is far from straightforward.

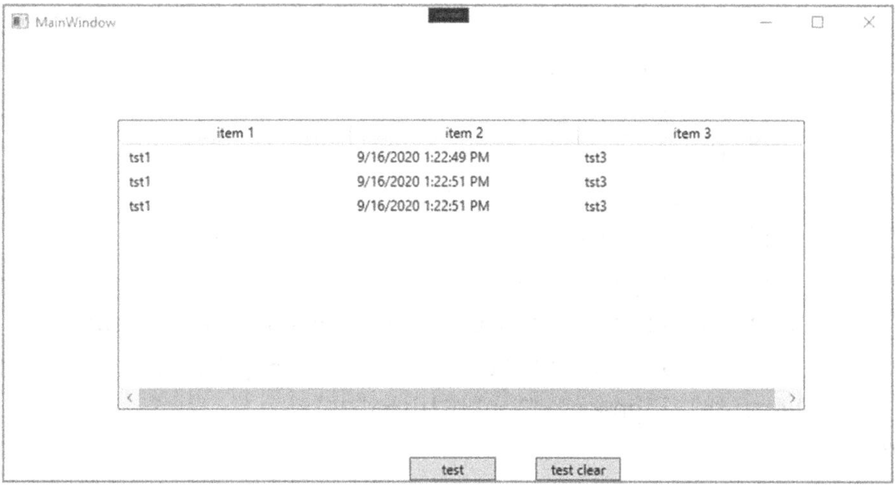

Figure 3-9. *ListView showcase*

Listing 3-19. XAML code for list view example

```
<Grid>
        <ListView MouseDoubleClick="lv_MouseDoubleClick"
        x:Name="lv" HorizontalAlignment="Left" Height="251"
        Margin="102,97,0,0" VerticalAlignment="Top"
        Width="602">
            <ListView.View>

                <GridView>
                    <GridViewColumn
                    DisplayMemberBinding="{Binding item1}"
                    Header="item 1" Width="200" />
                    <GridViewColumn
                    DisplayMemberBinding="{Binding item2}"
                    Header="item 2" Width="200" />
                    <GridViewColumn
                    DisplayMemberBinding="{Binding item3}"
                    Header="item 3" Width="200" />
                </GridView>
            </ListView.View>
        </ListView>
        <Button Click="Button_Click" Content="test"
        HorizontalAlignment="Left" Margin="358,389,0,0"
        VerticalAlignment="Top" Width="76"/>
        <Button Click="Button_Click_1" Content="test clear"
        HorizontalAlignment="Left" Margin="469,389,0,0"
        VerticalAlignment="Top" Width="75"/>
</Grid>
```

The way you interact with this is kind of MVVM based (which we will cover in Chapter 5). For the ListView itself (Figure 3-9, Listing 3-19), we have a name and an event, MouseDoubleClick, which will occur when the user double-clicks a specific item in the list. This can be useful for picking items from the list or displaying more details on that record. Basically, each record has columns or parts to it. The column goes into ListView.View; then in that, you have GridView, and each GridViewColumn is your column. Each column also contains something called DisplayMemberBinding, which is the most important piece here. We will have a class (a data model) which will contain item1, item2, and item3 properties – you will see how that makes sense in the C# code. With the list view, we also have a couple of buttons – one will clear the list and the other will add an item to the list.

Listing 3-20. C# code for the example

```csharp
public class TestBind
        {
            public string item1 { get; set; }
            public string item2 { get; set; }
            public string item3 { get; set; }

        private void Button_Click(object sender,
        RoutedEventArgs e)
        {
            var bnd = new TestBind();
            bnd.item1 = "tst1";
            bnd.item2 = DateTime.UtcNow.ToString();
            bnd.item3 = "tst3";

            lv.Items.Add(bnd);
        }

        private void Button_Click_1(object sender,
        RoutedEventArgs e)
        {
            lv.Items.Clear();
        }
```

```
private void lv_MouseDoubleClick(object sender,
MouseButtonEventArgs e)
{
    MessageBox.Show(((TestBind)((ListView)sender).
    SelectedItem).item2);
}
}
```

First, you may notice the class data model, which was mentioned previously. After that, we have a button click event in which we set one item to the list. What you need to do is construct your matching data model class and set the properties that you want displayed. After that, you use lv.Items.Add to add the object to the list. Once you know what to do, it is quite straightforward, but you still have to remember where to find everything. Unfortunately, retrieving the data is a little more complicated. For that, we can look at the third event method here, in which we display the double-clicked row's item2 in a message box (refer to the message box in Chapter 1). First of all, you need to access the sender object in the event (which is the ListView); from there, you get the SelectedItem property, and the selected value will be your data model class type; hence, you need to cast to that, and then you can access the properties. Finally, to clear the list, you simply need to use lv.Items.Clear() (see the second method).

Web Browser

The web browser element is by far not the most useful, and, if possible, it should not be used. If you need to redirect to a web page, the best way to do that is to redirect to a browser. However, this element is still being used sometimes, and it is useful to know how to deal with it.

Listing 3-21. XAML code for WebBrowser example

```
<Grid>
        <WebBrowser x:Name="wb" HorizontalAlignment="Left"
        Height="286" Margin="117,52,0,0"
        VerticalAlignment="Top" Width="561"/>
        <TextBox x:Name="urlbox" HorizontalAlignment="Left"
        Height="23" Margin="117,369,0,0" TextWrapping="Wrap"
        VerticalAlignment="Top" Width="355"/>
        <Button Click="Button_Click" Content="Go"
        HorizontalAlignment="Left" Margin="490,369,0,0"
        VerticalAlignment="Top" Width="74" Height="23"/>
</Grid>
```

In this arrangement, we simply have the WebBrowser element, a TextBox for the url, and a Button to load the url (See Listing 3-21).

Listing 3-22. Button click event for the example

```
private void Button_Click(object sender, RoutedEventArgs e)
        {
                var mainuri = new System.Uri(urlbox.Text);
                wb.Source = mainuri;
        }
```

Once you have the elements (See Listing 3-22), you can simply set the Source property of WebBrowser element (see Listing 3-22) and it will load. Other than that, it does not really do much, and it does not always work properly.

Canvas

Canvas element is a very specific one; you will either need it and it will be a centerpiece for the application or you will not need it. It is almost like a drawing board – you can use it for editing, drawing tools, or basic games.

75

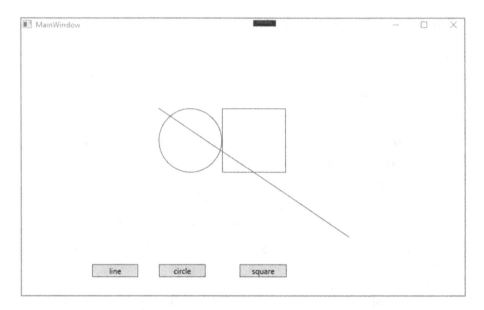

Figure 3-10. *Canvas with drawn shapes*

On the canvas (Figure 3-10), you need to draw elements, but more specifically, you need to add elements to the canvas. This example shows three buttons, which when clicked will draw a specific shape onto the canvas.

Listing 3-23. Canvas example in XAML

```
<Grid>
        <Canvas x:Name="cnv" HorizontalAlignment="Left"
        Height="200" Margin="225,115,0,0" VerticalAlignment="Top"
        Width="300"/>
        <Button Click="Line_bt_Click" x:Name="line_
        bt" Content="line" HorizontalAlignment="Left"
        Margin="118,358,0,0" VerticalAlignment="Top" Width="74"/>
        <Button Click="Circle_bt_Click" x:Name="circle_
        bt" Content="circle" HorizontalAlignment="Left"
        Margin="225,358,0,0" VerticalAlignment="Top" Width="74"/>
```

```
        <Button Click="Square_bt_Click" x:Name="square_
        bt" Content="square" HorizontalAlignment="Left"
        Margin="352,358,0,0" VerticalAlignment="Top" Width="74"/>
</Grid>
```

In the XAML (See Listing 3-23 and Figure 3-10), we have our canvas which has a name set, and it has a predefined height and width, which is especially important. Other than that, we have three buttons, and you will see the events accordingly.

Listing 3-24. Event for respective buttons

```
private void Line_bt_Click(object sender, RoutedEventArgs e)
        {
            Line ln = new Line();
            ln.Stroke = SystemColors.GrayTextBrush;
            ln.X1 = 0;
            ln.Y1 = 0;
            ln.X2 = 300;
            ln.Y2 = 200;
            cnv.Children.Add(ln);
        }

        private void Circle_bt_Click(object sender,
        RoutedEventArgs e)
        {
           Ellipse el = new Ellipse();
            el.Stroke = SystemColors.HighlightBrush;
            el.Width = 100;
            el.Height = 100;
            cnv.Children.Add(el);
        }
```

```
private void Square_bt_Click(object sender,
RoutedEventArgs e)
{
    Rectangle sq = new Rectangle();
    sq.Stroke = SystemColors.HighlightBrush;
    sq.Width = 100;
    sq.Height = 100;
    sq.Margin = new Thickness(100, 0, 0, 0);
    cnv.Children.Add(sq);
}
```

In the first event method (See Listing 3-24), you can see how the line is inserted (drawn). First, the line is a class, and it is constructed; once you have that Line object, you can set some properties. For the line and every other shape, you must set the Stroke property, which is the color. Another important thing is the coordinates; in the line, you need to set the start and end points. Ellipse and rectangle are a bit different; the ellipse height and width are basically the diameter – one value diameter from left to right (width) and the other from top to bottom (height). For the coordinates on those two items, you will need to use margin (relative to the canvas) and set the values using the Thickness type, where margins from the left will be as follows: left margin, top margin, right margin, and bottom margin. Finally, you need to add it to the children list in the canvas. In the next section, you will find that this process is very similar to adding other elements onto the grid.

Generate Elements in C#

Every drag and drop element in XAML also has a class in C#. So, you can actually generate your elements in C#, set the properties, and then add to the grid. This is good for when you need to do a list or some other dynamic operation, but unless necessary, it should be avoided as designing these elements can be tricky and time-consuming. The basic idea is quite simple – you need to construct it, add properties, and add elements to the grid, but there are still some things to watch out for.

Listing 3-25. Empty Grid for example

```
<Grid x:Name="maingrid">

</Grid>
```

Our example here will do something very simple – on a button click, it will take a value from a text box and display it in a message box. However, you may already have noticed that the grid (See Listing 3-25) is empty, and we have neither the button nor the text box. But you may also notice that we have a name for the grid – and to generate something is all you need.

Listing 3-26. The C# code for the example

```
public MainWindow()
      {
          InitializeComponent();
          GenerateElements();
      }

      void GenerateElements()
      {
          Button bt = new Button();
          //properties of button
          bt.Content = "Click to test";
          bt.Margin = new Thickness(10, 10, 0, 0);
          bt.HorizontalAlignment = HorizontalAlignment.Left;
          bt.VerticalAlignment = VerticalAlignment.Top;
          bt.Height = 30;
          bt.Width = 200;
          bt.Click += Bt_Click;
```

```
        TextBox tb = new TextBox();
        //properties of text box
        tb.Name = "tb1";
        tb.Margin = new Thickness(10, 60, 0, 0);
        tb.HorizontalAlignment = HorizontalAlignment.Left;
        tb.VerticalAlignment = VerticalAlignment.Top;
        tb.Height = 30;
        tb.Width = 200;

        maingrid.Children.Add(bt);
        maingrid.Children.Add(tb);
    }

    private void Bt_Click(object sender, RoutedEventArgs e)
    {
        var tb = maingrid.Children.OfType<TextBox>().
        First(Child => Child.Name == "tb1");
        MessageBox.Show(tb.Text);
    }
```

In this case, the C# part is the fun part of this whole arrangement (See Listing 3-26). First, we have a custom method in which we generate everything. You may also notice that is executed in the window constructor, after the InitializeComponent(), which is very important; otherwise, it will not work. We begin with the button, which is the Button class. Once constructed, you can set things like Content, Height, and other properties, but the most important ones are HorizontalAlignment, VerticalAlignment, and Margin; you really have to have these three for them to be displayed properly. The Margin is an interesting part; because of the way it is set, you need to use the Thickness type to set it. From left to right, Thickness will be left margin, top margin, right margin, and bottom margin. If you look at the example, the alignments are set at the left for horizontal and top for vertical; with that, we only care about the left and top margins. For the button, we also add a Click event which is especially important, and you can set any event for any element this way. Finally, the button and the text box are added to the grid; to do that, you need to access the Children property of the grid you want to add to and use the Add method by providing reference to the element object.

Background Tasks

If you run something within the event method, everything will be fine, but sometimes you need to run something in the background that is on a different thread. However, once you get into that new thread, the UI thread becomes inaccessible, and you need to access that to access the elements. Having said all that, there is a way to go around that issue, and it is not difficult at all.

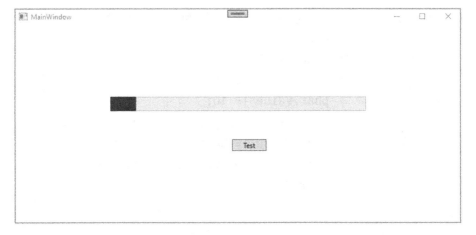

Figure 3-11. Progress bar loading

81

Listing 3-27. XAML code for the example

```
<Grid>
        <ProgressBar x:Name="pbar" HorizontalAlignment="Center"
        Height="25" Margin="0,123,0,0" VerticalAlignment="Top"
        Width="448"/>
        <Button Click="Button_Click" Content="Test"
        HorizontalAlignment="Left" Margin="382,197,0,0"
        VerticalAlignment="Top" Width="60"/>
</Grid>
```

In our example (See Listing 3-27), we have a progress bar and a button (see Figure 3-11). When a button is clicked, the progress bar will increase gradually, but the whole operation will happen in a background task.

Listing 3-28. C# code for the example

```
private async void Button_Click(object sender, RoutedEventArgs e)
        {
            _ = Task.Run(() => {
                Dispatcher.Invoke(async() => {
                    pbar.Value += 10;
                    await Task.Delay(5000);
                    pbar.Value += 50;
                    await Task.Delay(5000);
                    pbar.Value += 40;
                });
            });
            pbar.Foreground = new SolidColorBrush(Color.
            FromRgb(56, 20, 122));
        }
```

We use Task.Run (See Listing 3-28) without an await keyword to establish a background task; it does not interact with the UI thread, and with that, you cannot access any elements. We also change the color for the progress bar (See Figure 3-11), just so you can be sure that the task is in the background. To make this work, you have to wrap every procedure that interacts with the UI in a Dispatcher.Invoke method. Anything that is wrapped in that will work properly, and everything outside of it (in the background thread) will not.

CHAPTER 4

Files

At some point with any interface technology, you will have a need to pick a file or to save one. With WPF, this is likely to be even more common, as it is the perfect interface for handling files.

Pick and Save

When it comes to C#, to access a file, you basically need to establish a FileStream. In a console app, you do it by providing string for the directory, but in WPF, there is a more user-friendly way. Now, you can do something custom; you can also get a third party, but the best way is to use the built-in option to do it.

Listing 4-1. XAML arrangement for the file picker and destination selector example

```
<Grid>
        <Button x:Name="btpick" Click="Btpick_Click"
        Content="Pick..." HorizontalAlignment="Left"
        Margin="208,160,0,0" VerticalAlignment="Top"
        Width="119" Height="22"/>
        <Label   x:Name="pickedfilename"
        HorizontalAlignment="Left" Padding="0"
        Margin="332,160,0,0" VerticalAlignment="Top"
        Height="22" Width="183"/>
```

```
<Button x:Name="btsave" Click="Btsave_Click"
Content="Save as" HorizontalAlignment="Left"
Margin="208,219,0,0" VerticalAlignment="Top"
Width="119" Height="22"/>
</Grid>
```

In this example, we have two buttons (See Listing 4-1) – one will open the file picker, and the other will open the save dialog. With that, we have a label to display the file name. As you may already guess, WPF does not have any file picker or similar element, and with that, everything will be done in C#.

Listing 4-2. C# code for the initial setup

```
System.IO.Stream filestr;
    string file_ext = "";
    public MainWindow()
    {
        InitializeComponent();
    }
```

First, we need to establish a couple of variables (See Listing 4-2); one of them will be filestr, which is the FileStream for the picked file. The other one is called file_ext, which is the file extension, and although we do not display it anywhere, it will be useful to see how to retrieve it.

Listing 4-3. File picker button click event

```
private void Btpick_Click(object sender, RoutedEventArgs e)
    {
        var dialog = new Microsoft.Win32.OpenFileDialog();
        dialog.InitialDirectory = "D:\\test";
        if (dialog.ShowDialog() == true)
        {
            string tempname = dialog.FileName;
```

```
        var parsedname = tempname.Split('.');
        file_ext = parsedname[1];

        filestr = dialog.OpenFile();
        pickedfilename.Content = tempname;
    }
}
```

Now, the magic of file picking will be found in the Microsoft.Win32 namespace, where we pick the file we need to use OpenFileDialog (See Listing 4-3). At this point, the dialog only gets constructed; you can still set various properties to it to make it more user-friendly. We display the dialog using the ShowDialog method, and we put in an if statement because the file will only be picked if the user clicks OK, and with that, the return value will be true. Once we have the file picked, we can deal with it and its data. First, to get the name, you need to access the FileName property, but that will be the full file name (e.g., myfile.png); to get the name and extension separately, you need to split it at the dot. After that, we use the OpenFile method from the dialog to establish the FileStream for the picked file.

Listing 4-4. Button event for picking a file

```
private void Btsave_Click(object sender, RoutedEventArgs e)
        {
            var dialog = new Microsoft.Win32.SaveFileDialog();
            dialog.InitialDirectory = "D:\\test";
            dialog.Title = "Save as";
            dialog.FileName = "test";

            if (dialog.ShowDialog() == true)
            {
                string path = dialog.FileName;
                byte[] bytes = new byte[filestr.Length + 10];
                int numBytesToRead = (int)filestr.Length;
```

```
            int numBytesRead = 0;
            do
            {
                int n = filestr.Read(bytes,
                numBytesRead, 10);
                numBytesRead += n;
                numBytesToRead -= n;
            } while (numBytesToRead > 0);
            filestr.Close();

            System.IO.File.WriteAllBytes(path+"."+file_ext,
            bytes);

        }
    }
```

To save a file, you need to find an existing directory and establish the name for your new file. For that task, we use the SaveFileDialog method (See Listing 4-4) from Microsoft.Win32. With that, some dialog properties are initially set, and they are opened the same way as OpenFileDialog. The main difference here is that we do not retrieve a file stream; instead, we retrieve the FileName property, which is actually the full directory path with the file name at the end. After that, we have one of the ways you can write into the file, but you can feel free to choose other options available in C#. The only purpose SaveFileDialog serves is to pick the directory for the file to be saved – everything else is in your hands.

One more useful thing to know about file picker is the Filter property of the dialog. If set, it would allow only specified file types to be picked, and it can also be grouped.

Listing 4-5. File type filter

```
dialog.Filter = "Image files (*.bmp, *.jpg)|*.bmp;*.jpg|All
files (*.*)|*.*|Test filter (*.avi,*.png)|*.avi;*.png";
```

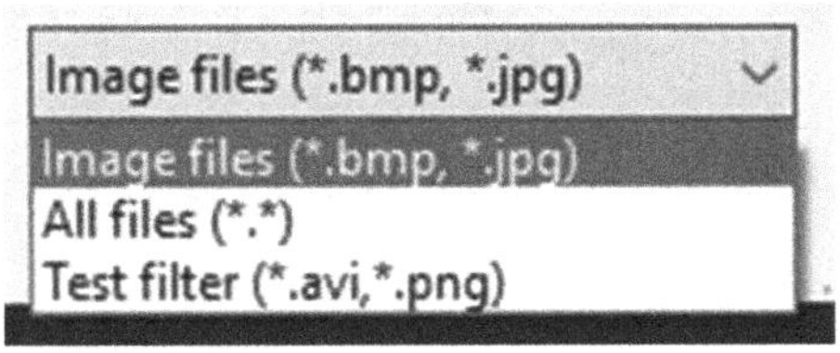

Figure 4-1. *File type filter drop-down in the file picker*

In this example (See Listing 4-5), we have three filter groups (Figure 4-1). To create a group, you first need a name "Image files"; then in parentheses, you have names for available extensions "(*.bmp, *.jpg)"; after that, you need to declare the extension in the same order that you have listed their names – "*.bmp;*.jpg".

Quick Example

This example is quite complex, but it achieves very simple yet very useful task – it takes an image file and then resizes it.

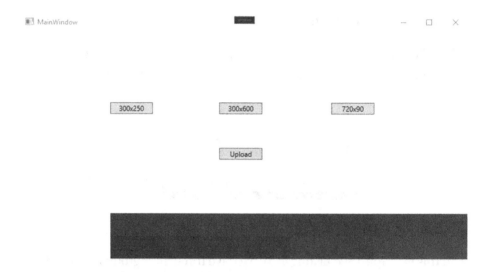

Figure 4-2. *Window view of the example after the size has been selected*

We have one button for picking the file and then three buttons which when clicked will resize the image to a predefined size (see Figure 4-2).

Listing 4-6. XAML code for the example

```
<Grid>
        <Button Content="Upload" HorizontalAlignment="Left"
        Margin="348,201,0,0" VerticalAlignment="Top" Width="75"
        Click="UploadButton_Click"/>
        <Button Content="300x250" HorizontalAlignment="Left"
        Margin="158,123,0,0" VerticalAlignment="Top" Width="75"
        Click="ResizeTo300x250_Click"/>
        <Button Content="300x600" HorizontalAlignment="Left"
        Margin="348,123,0,0" VerticalAlignment="Top" Width="75"
        Click="ResizeTo300x600_Click"/>
```

```
<Button Content="720x90" HorizontalAlignment="Left"
Margin="544,123,0,0" VerticalAlignment="Top" Width="75"
Click="ResizeTo720x90_Click"/>
<Image x:Name="previewbox" HorizontalAlignment="Left"
Margin="158,314,0,0" VerticalAlignment="Top"  />
</Grid>
```

In the XAML (See Figure 4-2, Listing 4-6), the arrangement is quite simple – we have four buttons and an Image element. Notice that the Image does not have width and height pre-set – that will be set according to which size is selected.

Listing 4-7. ImageResizer class

```
class ImageResizer
    {
        private readonly FileStream _OriginalFile;

        public ImageResizer(FileStream OriginalFile)
        {
            _OriginalFile = OriginalFile;
        }

        public BitmapImage Resize(int width, int height)
        {
            Image image = Image.FromStream(_OriginalFile);
            var destRect = new Rectangle(0, 0, width, height);
            var output = new Bitmap(width, height);

            output.SetResolution(image.HorizontalResolution,
            image.VerticalResolution);

            using (var gr = Graphics.FromImage(output))
            {
                gr.CompositingMode = CompositingMode.SourceCopy;
```

```
            gr.CompositingQuality = CompositingQuality.
            HighQuality;
            gr.InterpolationMode = InterpolationMode.
            HighQualityBicubic;
            gr.SmoothingMode = SmoothingMode.HighQuality;
            gr.PixelOffsetMode = PixelOffsetMode.
            HighQuality;

            using (var wrapMode = new ImageAttributes())
            {
                wrapMode.SetWrapMode(WrapMode.TileFlipXY);
                gr.DrawImage(image, destRect, 0, 0, image.
                Width, image.Height, GraphicsUnit.Pixel,
                wrapMode);
            }
        }
        image.Dispose();
        return ToBitmapImage(output);
    }

    private  BitmapImage ToBitmapImage(Bitmap bitmap)
    {
        using (var memory = new MemoryStream())
        {
            bitmap.Save(memory, ImageFormat.Png);
            memory.Position = 0;

            var bitmapImage = new BitmapImage();
            bitmapImage.BeginInit();
            bitmapImage.StreamSource = memory;
            bitmapImage.CacheOption = BitmapCacheOption.
            OnLoad;
```

```
            bitmapImage.EndInit();
            bitmapImage.Freeze();

            return bitmapImage;
        }
    }
}
```

This ImageResizer class (See Listing 4-7) will handle the resizing of the image. This is not exactly WPF specific, but it may not work on other arrangements.

Listing 4-8. Using statements for the ImageResizer class

```
using System.Drawing;
using System.Drawing.Drawing2D;
using System.Drawing.Imaging;
using System.Windows.Media.Imaging;
```

For this to work, you will need to use these using statements (See Listing 4-8). The constructor here takes the FileStream and sets it for later use. We also have a method called ToBitmapImage; this is what gets displayed, but when you resize graphics, you only get Bitmap. To resize an image, we need to establish the Image type variable from the FileStream; then we create a Bitmap and Rectangle for the specified width and height. Graphics type is basically where you deal with quality and then export the new image using the DrawImage method. To convert Bitmap to BitmapImage, you need to get the data from Bitmap to a memory stream and then set that value to BitmapImage StreamSource.

Listing 4-9. C# contents of MainWindow.xaml.cs

```csharp
public MainWindow()
        {
            InitializeComponent();
        }

        ImageResizer resizer;

        private void UploadButton_Click(object sender,
        RoutedEventArgs e)
        {
            var dialog = new Microsoft.Win32.OpenFileDialog();
            dialog.InitialDirectory = "D:\\test";
            if (dialog.ShowDialog() == true)
            {
                resizer = new ImageResizer(new System.
                IO.FileStream(dialog.FileName,System.
                IO.FileMode.Open));

            }
        }

        private void ResizeTo300x250_Click(object sender,
        RoutedEventArgs e)
        {
            previewbox.Source = resizer.Resize(300, 250);
        }

        private void ResizeTo300x600_Click(object sender,
        RoutedEventArgs e)
        {
            previewbox.Source = resizer.Resize(300, 600);
        }
```

```
private void ResizeTo720x90_Click(object sender,
RoutedEventArgs e)
{
    previewbox.Source = resizer.Resize(720, 90);
}
```

Now that you know how the resizer works, we can get back to the WPF part (See Listing 4-9), and since most of the hard work is handled at the ImageResizer class, there is not much to find in the window. First, we must deal with the upload button, which simply uses OpenFileDialog to pick the files and then establishes an ImageResizer object which takes in the file reference. After that, we have three different buttons – they all execute the Resize method and set the return value to previewbox (Image element) Source property. This is the reason why we have to convert from Bitmap to BitmapImage, as that is the type that the Source property requires.

Quick Exercise

Your task is to create a program, which will take an Image file, establish a new name in a specified format, and allow to save the file with the new name. You should also add a progress bar for selecting the file and generating a new name.

Name format: {image width}X{image height}T{time stamp}

Exclude the curly brackets from the name.

Listing 4-10. Image class setup

```
System.Drawing.Image image = System.Drawing.Image.
FromStream(FileStream);
```

Use this code (see Listing 4-10) to access the image data.

Figure 4-3. *Example window view after the file has been selected*

As you can see (Figure 4-3), the application allows the user to select a file, preview the name once selected, and then save it.

Listing 4-11. The XAML layout for the example

```
<Grid>
        <Button x:Name="SelectFileBt"  Click="SelectFileBt_
        Click" Content="Select file..."
        HorizontalAlignment="Left" Margin="219,116,0,0"
        VerticalAlignment="Top" Width="75"/>
        <Button x:Name="SaveFileBt" Click="SaveFileBt_Click"
        Content="Save As.." HorizontalAlignment="Left"
        Margin="450,116,0,0" VerticalAlignment="Top"
        Width="75"/>
        <Label Content="Original name:"
        HorizontalAlignment="Left" Margin="220,218,0,0"
        VerticalAlignment="Top"/>
        <Label x:Name="OrginalName" Content=""
        HorizontalAlignment="Left" Margin="323,218,0,0"
        VerticalAlignment="Top" Width="202"/>
```

```
<Label Content="New name:" HorizontalAlignment="Left"
Margin="237,266,0,0" VerticalAlignment="Top"
Width="70"/>
<Label x:Name="NewName" Content=""
HorizontalAlignment="Left" Margin="323,266,0,0"
VerticalAlignment="Top" Width="202"/>
<ProgressBar x:Name="ProgressBar"
HorizontalAlignment="Left" Height="9"
Margin="219,160,0,0" VerticalAlignment="Top"
Width="306"/>
</Grid>
```

The XAML part (See Figure 4-3 and Listing 4-11) is quite straightforward; we have two buttons with two events for them. We also have some labels to show where things are and to display values. Finally, we have a progress bar.

Listing 4-12. Initial setup for the example

```
public MainWindow()
        {
            InitializeComponent();
        }

        Stream SelectedFile;
        string SelectedFileExtension;
```

Before anything else, we need to set two variables (See Listing 4-12) – one for the selected file's FileStream and the other for the selected file's extension.

Listing 4-13. Select file dialog for the example

```
private void SelectFileBt_Click(object sender, RoutedEventArgs e)
        {
            var dialog = new Microsoft.Win32.OpenFileDialog();
            dialog.InitialDirectory = "D:\\test";
```

```
if (dialog.ShowDialog() == true)
{
    ProgressBar.IsIndeterminate = true;
    string tempname = dialog.FileName;

    var parsedname = tempname.Split('.');
    SelectedFileExtension = parsedname[1];
    OrginalName.Content = (parsedname[0].
    Split('\\')).Last();
    SelectedFile = dialog.OpenFile();

    System.Drawing.Image image = System.Drawing.
    Image.FromStream(SelectedFile);
    NewName.Content = image.Width + "x" + image.
    Height+ "T" + DateTime.UtcNow.Ticks.ToString();
    image.Dispose();
    ProgressBar.IsIndeterminate = false;
}
}
```

After the variables are established, we can deal with picking the file (See Listing 4-13). For the most part, this is just a generic file picker arrangement. We set the FileStream to SelectedFile and also set the SelectedFileExtension. To get the image size, we establish a new Image variable, and from it, we can retrieve the width and height of the image. With all that, we also have a progress bar IsIndeterminate set to true in the beginning and to false at the end.

Listing 4-14. Save file dialog for the example

```
private void SaveFileBt_Click(object sender, RoutedEventArgs e)
    {
        var dialog = new Microsoft.Win32.
        SaveFileDialog();
        dialog.InitialDirectory = "D:\\test";
```

```
dialog.Title = "Save as";
dialog.FileName = NewName.Content.ToString()+".
"+SelectedFileExtension;

if (dialog.ShowDialog() == true)
{
    string path = dialog.FileName;
    SelectedFile.Seek(0, SeekOrigin.Begin);
    byte[] bytes = new byte[SelectedFile.Length
    + 10];
    int numBytesToRead = (int)SelectedFile.
    Length;
    int numBytesRead = 0;
    do
    {
        int n = SelectedFile.Read(bytes,
        numBytesRead, 10);
        numBytesRead += n;
        numBytesToRead -= n;
    } while (numBytesToRead > 0);
    SelectedFile.Close();

    System.IO.File.WriteAllBytes(path, bytes);
}
}
```

The next step is to save the file (See Listing 4-14), and since all the "hard work" was done in the selecting phase, there is not much to do here. Do note, however, that in this case we need to Seek the FileStream to the beginning as it was used by the Image.FromStream method.

CHAPTER 5

MVVM

Although MVVM is a structure that we can represent in drawings and diagrams, what you really need to know is the way to handle events and other things in the WPF. Before jumping into the examples, we need to take a look at some theory and how this arrangement can be used.

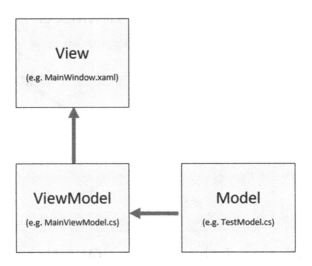

Figure 5-1. *Basic representation of MVVM*

The View in the MVVM is the XAML file (either for window or for page). The main idea here is not to use the code-behind file; instead, we have the ViewModel file for handling those events and other arrangements. Then the Model is just a data model, a class with simple properties used as an object to describe something. Take a look at

© Taurius Litvinavicius 2021
T. Litvinavicius, *Exploring Windows Presentation Foundation*,
https://doi.org/10.1007/978-1-4842-6637-3_5

Figure 5-1; it basically shows what can access what and which elements of MVVM would represent which files in a WPF project.

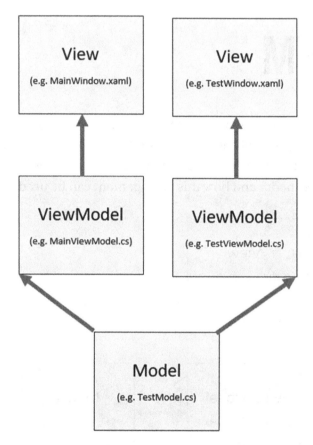

Figure 5-2. *More complex representation of MVVM*

A ViewModel is not necessarily bound to one single view (see Figure 5-2); it can be applied to several views, although such arrangement may not be very common. On the other, the same model can be applied on many ViewModels.

The MVVM structure should be avoided if possible; usually it is not necessary, and it will simply waste your time. As you will see in the code, there is a lot more of it for the same simple procedures that could be done with a lot less code in simple events. Also, if you are going to use this arrangement, you do not have to use it on every window and every page (See Figure 5-2). Having said all that, many of the existing WPF applications use this in at least some way, so it is useful to know how everything works.

Element to Element Binding

The idea of this basic binding is to bind the input of an element to another element which is capable to output the value. In this case, we will be looking at the TextBox element binding with a TextBlock (see Figure 5-3); in other words, it is like setting the Text property of the TextBlock with a value from the Text property of the TextBox.

Figure 5-3. *Example of interface view*

Listing 5-1. XAML code for the example

```
<Grid>
        <TextBox x:Name="tb" HorizontalAlignment="Left"
        Margin="194,85,0,0" Text="" TextWrapping="Wrap"
        VerticalAlignment="Top" Width="162" Height="29"/>
        <TextBlock DataContext="{x:Reference Name=tb}"
        Text="{Binding Path=Text}" HorizontalAlignment="Left"
        Margin="194,144,0,0"   TextWrapping="Wrap"
        VerticalAlignment="Top" Height="27" Width="162"/>
</Grid>
```

In such an arrangement, everything is done in XAML (See Listing 5-1). The TextBox element does need a name for referencing, but we reference that in one of the TextBlock properties – DataContext. This basically sets the source of data for the TextBlock, but then you still need to specify that in the Text property by setting Path to Text.

Introducing ViewModel

Although we will be looking at the ViewModel part of MVVM arrangement, the main goal here is to understand how to bind data from input to a variable and then how to deal with simple events in a different way than declaring an event.

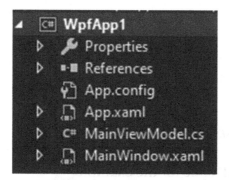

Figure 5-4. *File layout for the example*

The ViewModel is a class, but it should always be associated with a view (it might be a window or a page). In this case, we have MainWindow, and for it, we have MainViewModel – you can see (Figure 5-4) how the word Main matched in both names. Functionality wise, this is not required, but it is easier to follow the structure.

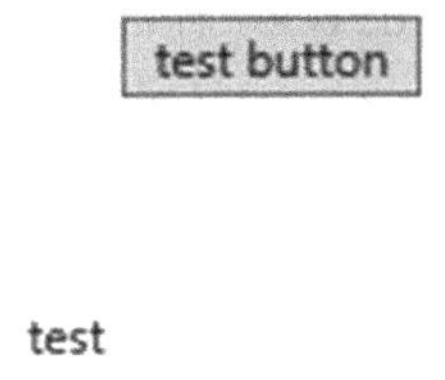

test button

test

Figure 5-5. *First state of the example*

Initially, the page has a button and displays the word "test" in a TextBlock (see Figure 5-5).

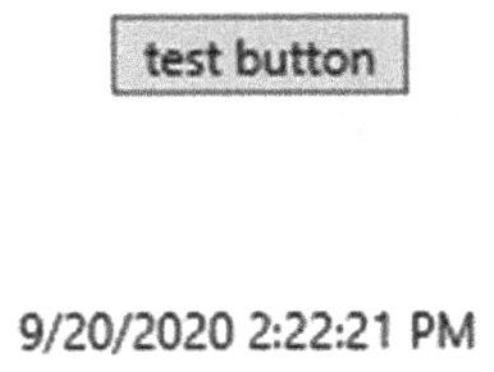

test button

9/20/2020 2:22:21 PM

Figure 5-6. *Second state of the example*

After the button is clicked, it will display a current date and time (see Figure 5-6).

Listing 5-2. ViewModel for the main window (MainWindow.xaml)

```
using System;
using System.ComponentModel;
using System.Windows.Input;

namespace WpfApp1
{
    public class MainViewModel : INotifyPropertyChanged
    {
        public event PropertyChangedEventHandler
        PropertyChanged;
```

```
private ICommand _clickCommand;
public string PropertyForLabel { get; set; } = "test";
public ICommand ClickCommand
{
    get
    {
        return _clickCommand ?? (_clickCommand = new
        CommandHandler(() => TestAction(), () =>
        CanExecute));
    }
}
public bool CanExecute
{
    get
    {
        return true;
    }
}

public void TestAction()
{

    PropertyForLabel = DateTime.UtcNow.ToString();
    PropertyChanged.Invoke(this, new PropertyChanged
    EventArgs("PropertyForLabel"));
}
}

public class CommandHandler : ICommand
{
    private Action _action;
    private Func<bool> _canExecute;
```

```csharp
    public CommandHandler(Action action, Func<bool>
    canExecute)
    {
        _action = action;
        _canExecute = canExecute;
    }

    public event EventHandler CanExecuteChanged
    {
        add { CommandManager.RequerySuggested += value; }
        remove { CommandManager.RequerySuggested -= value; }
    }

    public bool CanExecute(object parameter)
    {
        return _canExecute.Invoke();
    }

    public void Execute(object parameter)
    {
        _action();
    }
    }
}
```

We must first look at the ViewModel (See Listing 5-2), which actually
is a class, in a way. It is, however, quite a complicated class, and you need
to see the whole thing. The using statements are crucial here, and in the
namespace, we not only have the MainViewModel class, but we also have
another one – CommandHandler.

The MainViewModel class has a few things going on, but actually,
there are only two things that we have here. We have a string property,
PropertyForLabel, which holds the value displayed in the TextBlock.

Then we have ClickCommand and _ClickCommand, which are for the click event on the button. Most of this is quite generic, but as you can see, there is quite a lot of code. ClickCommand has a get attribute set, which basically returns a newly constructed CommandHandler. Now, the command handler is basically what handles the event itself, and the code you see is quite generic. In customizing something, you deal with the action – the first parameter of the CommandHandler constructor method. You also have a method which returns a Boolean on whether the event can execute or not; in this case, it would always execute, but if you need to add something, you can do that in the CanExecute method, and if you do not want it to execute under a certain scenario, simply return false.

So, in this arrangement, when the button is clicked, the TestAction method will be executed. What we are doing here is something called TwoWay binding; if something changes in the TextBox, then the same is applied to the variable. Then if the variable is set, the TextBlock value will change as well. For this to work, you actually need to notify the user interface. So, in the method, we first assign the date to the variable and then PropertyChanged.Invoke to notify the user interface about the change. INotifyPropertyChanged is required for this to work.

Listing 5-3. XAML code for the example

```
<Grid>
        <Button Command="{Binding ClickCommand}" Content="test
        button" HorizontalAlignment="Left" Margin="344,179,0,0"
        VerticalAlignment="Top" Width="75"/>
        <TextBlock  Text="{Binding PropertyForLabel,
        Mode=TwoWay, UpdateSourceTrigger=PropertyChanged}"
        HorizontalAlignment="Left" Margin="320,250,0,0"
        VerticalAlignment="Top" Width="149"/>
</Grid>
```

For the whole arrangement to work, you still need to take some actions in the XAML code (See Listing 5-3). First, you need to set the Command property of the button – in this case, we specify ClickCommand as our command. The TextBlock is a bit more complicated; you need to set the Text property, where you provide the property that we had in the class, and then a Mode of binding, and finally you set UpdateSourceTrigger which in this case is PropertyChanged, and you may notice that it corresponds with the PropertyChanged.Invoke method.

Listing 5-4. C# code for the code-behind file

```
public MainWindow()
      {
          DataContext = new MainViewModel();
          InitializeComponent();
      }
```

The final and probably the most important thing is to set DataContext in the window constructor (see Listing 5-4). The context is the ViewModel, and if not set, nothing will work.

Implementing Models

You have already seen how a view (A Window) interacts with a ViewModel; now it is time to see how a data model will come into the equation. Our example will mainly focus on a ListView (it was covered in Chapter 3, Section 9), but it will be in full MVVM structure.

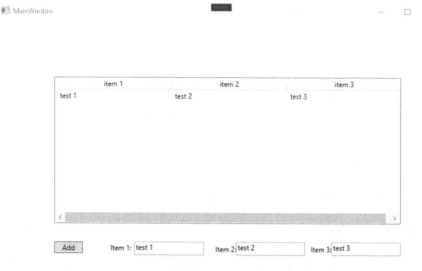

Figure 5-7. *View for the example*

The example (see Figure 5-7) has a ListView, three text boxes, and a button which when clicked adds values from text boxes to the list view.

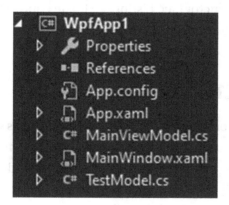

Figure 5-8. *File layout for the example*

In this case, alongside the MainWindow (See Figure 5-7), we have the MainViewModel and TestModel class (see Figure 5-8). You may notice that the model class name does correspond with the Window name.

110

This is because the model is not directly associated with the view or the ViewModel; hence, the name should correspond to whatever data the model represents.

Listing 5-5. MainViewModel for the MainWindow

```
public class MainViewModel : INotifyPropertyChanged
    {
        public event PropertyChangedEventHandler
        PropertyChanged;

        private ICommand _clickCommand;
        public ObservableCollection<TestModel> TestViewData {
        get; set; } = new ObservableCollection<TestModel>();
        public string InputItem1 { get; set; }
        public string InputItem2 { get; set; }
        public string InputItem3 { get; set; }
        public ICommand ClickCommand
        {
            get
            {
                return _clickCommand ?? (_clickCommand = new
                CommandHandler(() => InsertAction(), () =>
                CanExecute));
            }
        }
        public bool CanExecute
        {
            get
            {
                return true;
            }
        }
```

```
    public void InsertAction()
    {
        TestViewData.Add(new TestModel() { item1 =
        InputItem1, item2 = InputItem2, item3 = InputItem3
        });
        PropertyChanged.Invoke(this, new PropertyChanged
        EventArgs("TestViewData"));
    }

}

public class CommandHandler : ICommand
{
    private Action _action;
    private Func<bool> _canExecute;

    public CommandHandler(Action action, Func<bool>
    canExecute)
    {
        _action = action;
        _canExecute = canExecute;
    }

    public event EventHandler CanExecuteChanged
    {
        add { CommandManager.RequerySuggested += value; }
        remove { CommandManager.RequerySuggested -= value; }
    }

    public bool CanExecute(object parameter)
    {
        return _canExecute.Invoke();
    }
```

```
    public void Execute(object parameter)
    {
        _action();
    }
}
```

Just like in the previous example (ViewModel section), we have a CommandHandler, which is exactly the same as previously (See Listing 5-5). The same goes for the ClickCommand and _clickCommand properties. The difference starts with the TestViewData, which is something called ObservableCollection. Now that is basically a list, but it is a list specifically for the ListView element. We also have three string properties, which we will bind to the text boxes accordingly.

Listing 5-6. Data model for the example

```
public class TestModel
    {
        public string item1 { get; set; }
        public string item2 { get; set; }
        public string item3 { get; set; }
    }
```

The model in this case is an item for that list in the ListView element (See Listing 5-6).

At this point, we have covered the properties that we have in the ListView, the generic stuff that exists there. All that is left now is to look at the InsertAction, and then we can go to XAML. In this case, we simply need to add new model object to the list, and just like we did previously, we need to notify the UI that something has changed.

Listing 5-7. XAML code for the example

```
<Grid>
        <ListView  x:Name="lv" HorizontalAlignment="Left"
        ItemsSource="{Binding TestViewData, Mode=TwoWay, Up
        dateSourceTrigger=PropertyChanged}" Height="251"
        Margin="102,97,0,0" VerticalAlignment="Top"
        Width="602">
            <ListView.View>

                <GridView>
                    <GridViewColumn
                    DisplayMemberBinding="{Binding item1}"
                    Header="item 1" Width="200" />
                    <GridViewColumn
                    DisplayMemberBinding="{Binding item2}"
                    Header="item 2" Width="200" />
                    <GridViewColumn
                    DisplayMemberBinding="{Binding item3}"
                    Header="item 3" Width="200" />
                </GridView>
            </ListView.View>
        </ListView>
        <Button Content="Add" Command="{Binding ClickCommand}"
        HorizontalAlignment="Left" Margin="102,379,0,0"
        VerticalAlignment="Top" Width="50"/>
        <TextBox Text="{Binding InputItem1}"
        HorizontalAlignment="Left" Height="23"
        Margin="242,379,0,0" TextWrapping="Wrap"
        VerticalAlignment="Top" Width="120"/>
```

```
<TextBox Text="{Binding InputItem2}"
HorizontalAlignment="Left" Height="23"
Margin="418,379,0,0" TextWrapping="Wrap"
VerticalAlignment="Top" Width="120"/>
<TextBox Text="{Binding InputItem3}"
HorizontalAlignment="Left" Height="23"
Margin="584,379,0,0" TextWrapping="Wrap"
VerticalAlignment="Top" Width="120"/>
<TextBlock HorizontalAlignment="Left"
Margin="201,381,0,0" TextWrapping="Wrap" Text="Item 1:"
VerticalAlignment="Top"/>
<TextBlock HorizontalAlignment="Left"
Margin="382,383,0,0" TextWrapping="Wrap" Text="Item 2:"
VerticalAlignment="Top"/>
<TextBlock HorizontalAlignment="Left"
Margin="548,383,0,0" TextWrapping="Wrap" Text="Item 3:"
VerticalAlignment="Top"/>
</Grid>
```

First, we may look at the ListView (See Listing 5-7), which in this case has used our TestModel for binding. Initially, you need to set ItemsSource – that is the object which contains properties, the same as you have seen before in Chapter 3. Once that is done, you can basically distribute properties to the GridViewColumn items, again the same as you would do in regular ListView. After that, we assign ClickCommand to the "Add" button. Also, we have our InputItem1 and the others connected to the text boxes, and since we do not need two-way binding, we neither need to set it as two-way binding nor we need to notify the UI (see Listing 5-5) about the change.

Quick Example

In this example, you will see a WPF application that implements an API which lets the user access the country "database". The whole arrangement is quite simple, but our goal here is to explore how MVVM structure works and how modern ways of retrieving data from API can help you save time and make your code more readable.

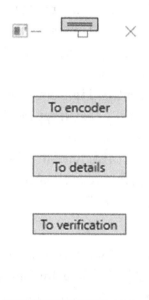

Figure 5-9. *Main window for the example*

Initially, we have three navigation options for the program in the main window (see Figure 5-9).

Figure 5-10. *Encoder window*

The first feature is the basic encoder (see Figure 5-10); it either converts country code to name or name to country code. We use a tab view to separate the two options.

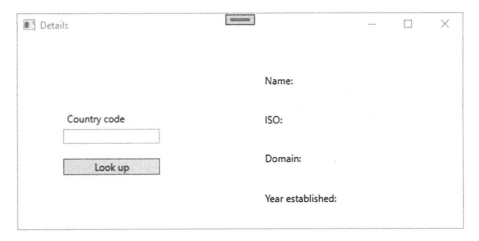

Figure 5-11. *Look up window*

The second feature is the retrieval of country information (see Figure 5-11) – name, ISO code, domain, and year it was established.

117

Figure 5-12. *Verification window*

Finally, we have the verification feature (see Figure 5-12) – this lets the user enter the country data and verify it against the database records.

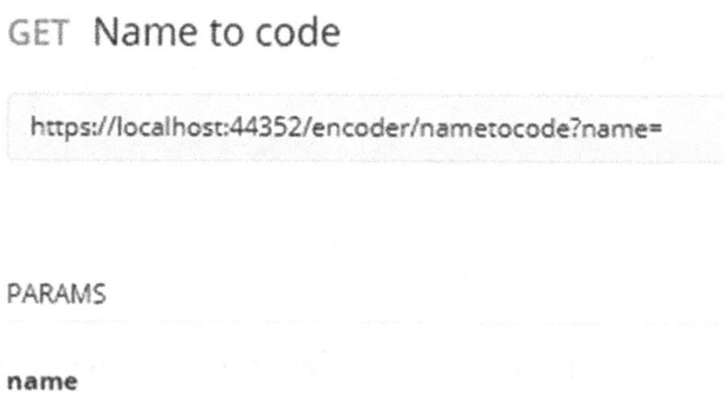

Figure 5-13. *API documentation – name to code*

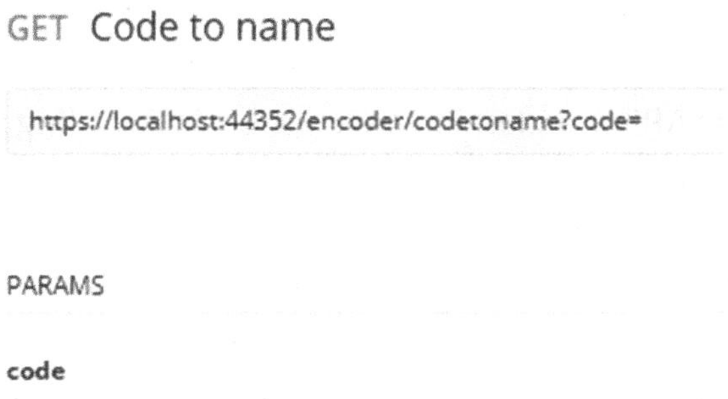

GET Code to name

https://localhost:44352/encoder/codetoname?code=

PARAMS

code

Figure 5-14. *API documentation – name to code*

GET full details

https://localhost:44352/details/full?countrycode=AD

PARAMS

countrycode   AD

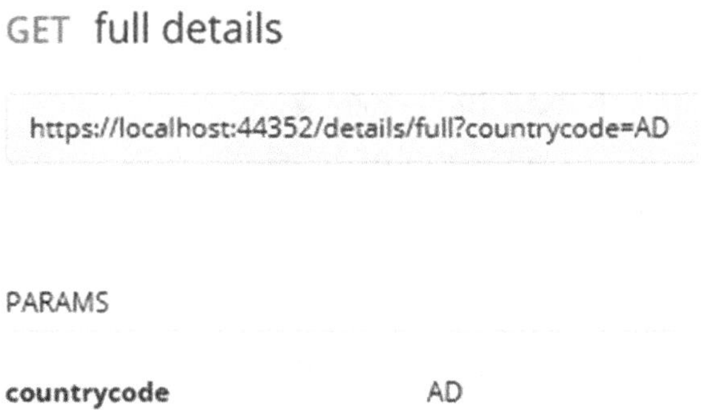

Figure 5-15. *API documentation – name to code*

POST verify

https://localhost:44352/details/verify

BODY raw

```
{"code":"AD","country":"Andorra","year established":1974,"domain"
```

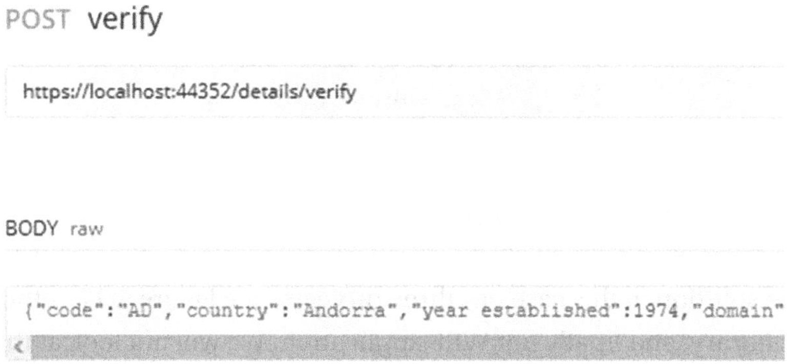

Figure 5-16. *API documentation – name to code*

The idea here is to implement the API according to the documentation; the application itself can have many arrangements, but it cannot go beyond what the API provides. First, we see basic encoding routes in the API (see Figures 5-12 and 5-13); a string is sent in parameters, and another string is retrieved. With that, we have the third route (see Figure 5-15), which will retrieve the country details according to the country code provided. Finally, we have the verification route (see Figure 5-16), which takes the country data model object (you will see that later) and verifies its content against the records.

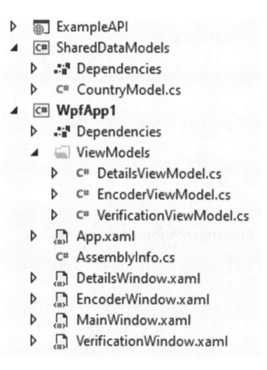

Figure 5-17. *File layout for the example project*

The solution in this case has three projects (see Figure 5-17) – the API, a code library, and finally our WPF application. We will not look at the API, as the goal here is to only see how it is implemented. In the WPF project, you may notice that we have a ViewModels folder; it is always better to keep ViewModels and Models in a separate directory so that you could find everything quickly. Now, we have the ViewModel arrangement for the three main features, but we will leave the traditional events for the MainWindow.

Listing 5-8. XAML code for the MainWindow

```
<Grid>
        <Button x:Name="bt_toencoder" Click="bt_
        toencoder_Click" Content="To encoder"
        HorizontalAlignment="Center" Margin="0,46,0,0"
        VerticalAlignment="Top" Width="90"/>
        <Button x:Name="bt_todetails" Click="bt_
        todetails_Click" Content="To details"
        HorizontalAlignment="Center" Margin="0,103,0,0"
        VerticalAlignment="Top" Width="90"/>
        <Button x:Name="bt_toverification" Click="bt_
        toverification_Click" Content="To verification"
        HorizontalAlignment="Center" Margin="0,158,0,0"
        VerticalAlignment="Top" Width="90"/>
</Grid>
```

The main window simply contains the buttons for the associated events.

Listing 5-9. C# code for the MainWindow

```
private void bt_toencoder_Click(object sender, RoutedEventArgs e)
        {
            (new EncoderWindow()).Show();
        }
```

```
private void bt_todetails_Click(object sender,
RoutedEventArgs e)
{
    (new DetailsWindow()).Show();
}

private void bt_toverification_Click(object sender,
RoutedEventArgs e)
{
    (new VerificationWindow()).Show();
}
```

In the C# part for the MainWindow (See Listing 5-9), we simply open an appropriate window for each event. Do notice how in this case we do not assign the constructed windows to a new variable; instead, we execute the Show method right away.

Listing 5-10. Country data model

```
public class CountryModel
    {
        public string Code { get; set; }

        public string Country { get; set; }

        [JsonPropertyName("year established")]
        [JsonProperty("year established")]
        public long? YearEstablished { get; set; }

        public string Domain { get; set; }

        [JsonPropertyName("iso code")]
        [JsonProperty("iso code")]
        public string IsoCode { get; set; }
```

```
public string Description { get; set; }
}
```

The country model (See Listing 5-10) will get more attention in this case, as it is not as basic as model classes usually are. In this case, we use the JsonPropertyName and JsonProperty attributes; we do this because the name in json has a space, and with that, it cannot correspond with the variable in C#. The reason we have to use both of them in this case is because one of them will work in the HttpClient (in the WPF part) and the other one will only work for the API.

Listing 5-11. App.xaml.cs for the example

```
public partial class App : Application
    {
        public static HttpClient client = new HttpClient() {
        BaseAddress = new Uri("https://localhost:44352") };
    }
```

In the App.xaml.cs file (See Listing 5-11), we have a static HttpClient, which will handle the API access in our program. But there will be one more thing that will need to be referenced in order for this to work in a modern way.

Listing 5-12. Contents for DetailsViewModel.cs

```
class DetailsViewModel : INotifyPropertyChanged
    {
        public event PropertyChangedEventHandler
        PropertyChanged;

        private ICommand _clickCommand;

        public SharedDataModels.CountryModel Country { get;
        set; } = new SharedDataModels.CountryModel();
```

```csharp
public ICommand ClickCommand
{
    get
    {
        return _clickCommand ?? (_clickCommand
        = new CommandHandler(async () => await
        LookupActionAsync(), () => CanExecute));
    }
}
public bool CanExecute
{
    get
    {
        return true;
    }
}

public async Task LookupActionAsync()
{
    try
    {
        Country = await App.client.GetFromJsonAsync
        <SharedDataModels.CountryModel>("/details/
        full?countrycode=" + Country.Code);
        PropertyChanged.Invoke(this, new PropertyChanged
        EventArgs("Country"));
    }
    catch (Exception ex)
    {
        MessageBox.Show(ex.Message);
    }
}
```

```
}

public class CommandHandler : ICommand
{
    private Action _action;
    private Func<bool> _canExecute;

    public CommandHandler(Action action, Func<bool>
    canExecute)
    {
        _action = action;
        _canExecute = canExecute;
    }

    public event EventHandler CanExecuteChanged
    {
        add { CommandManager.RequerySuggested += value; }
        remove { CommandManager.RequerySuggested -= value; }
    }

    public bool CanExecute(object parameter)
    {
        return _canExecute.Invoke();
    }

    public void Execute(object parameter)
    {
        _action();
    }
}
```

We will first look at the details feature (See Listing 5-12), as it is more straightforward than the other ones. We have the ViewModel class and the CommandHandler, but notice that the whole thing is in the

ViewModels namespace, and with that, the CommandHandler will only be declared here, not in the other ViewModels. In the main class here, we have a CountryModel property declared. We will not use any additional variables; instead, we will bind data directly to the model class properties. With that, we also have ClickCommand, which basically executes the LookupActionAsync method. The difference from what you saw before is that the method here is a task method, which then requires to be awaited.

The Country property in this case or any property used for binding must be public. Otherwise, nothing will work, and you will also see no error message.

Listing 5-13. using statements for the example

```
using System.Net.Http.Json;
using System.Windows;
```

For this arrangement to work, we will need a couple of using statements (See Listing 5-13). The first one is for the API calls; the HttpClient requires this to be there if you want to use GetFromJsonAsync and other Json-related methods.

The second using statement is for the MessageBox; in a window or a page, you have this by default. But in a normal class, which is what the ViewModel is, the using statement for the namespace needs to be declared.

Listing 5-14. XAML code for the country details lookup

```xml
<Grid>
        <TextBox Text="{Binding Country.Code,
        Mode=TwoWay, UpdateSourceTrigger=PropertyChang
        ed}" HorizontalAlignment="Left" Margin="57,145,0,0"
        TextWrapping="Wrap" VerticalAlignment="Top"
        Width="120"/>
        <Label Content="Country code"
        HorizontalAlignment="Left" Margin="57,119,0,0"
        VerticalAlignment="Top" Width="98"/>
        <Label Content="Name:"  HorizontalAlignment="Left"
        Margin="302,73,0,0" VerticalAlignment="Top"
        Width="98"/>
        <Label Content="ISO:" HorizontalAlignment="Left"
        Margin="302,121,0,0" VerticalAlignment="Top"
        Width="98"/>
        <Label Content="Domain:" HorizontalAlignment="Left"
        Margin="302,168,0,0" VerticalAlignment="Top"
        Width="98"/>
        <Label Content="Year established:"
        HorizontalAlignment="Left" Margin="302,217,0,0"
        VerticalAlignment="Top" Width="98"/>
        <Button  Command="{Binding ClickCommand}" Content="Look
        up" HorizontalAlignment="Left" Margin="57,181,0,0"
        VerticalAlignment="Top" Width="120"/>
        <Label Content="{Binding Country.Country}"
        HorizontalAlignment="Left" Margin="400,73,0,0"
        VerticalAlignment="Top" Width="98" Height="26"/>
        <Label Content="{Binding Country.IsoCode}"
        HorizontalAlignment="Left" Margin="400,119,0,0"
        VerticalAlignment="Top" Width="98" Height="26"/>
```

```
<Label Content="{Binding Country.Domain}"
HorizontalAlignment="Left" Margin="400,168,0,0"
VerticalAlignment="Top" Width="98" Height="26"/>
<Label Content="{Binding Country.YearEstablished}"
HorizontalAlignment="Left" Margin="400,217,0,0"
VerticalAlignment="Top" Width="98" Height="26"/>
</Grid>
```

In the XAML code (See Listing 5-14), we need to bind the elements to some of these properties. The idea here is mainly the same as you saw in the initial examples of MVVM, but there is one difference. We are taking properties from the class model object, and to do that, you basically need to declare the full route to the property, for example, Country.Domain.

Listing 5-15. Constructor in DetailsWindow.xaml.cs

```
public DetailsWindow()
        {
            DataContext = new ViewModels.DetailsViewModel();
            InitializeComponent();
        }
```

Finally, you must never forget to set the DataContext in the constructor for the window (See Listing 5-15). This is crucial to do, and it is also very easy to miss.

Listing 5-16. EncoderViewModel contents

```
class EncoderViewModel : INotifyPropertyChanged
    {
        public event PropertyChangedEventHandler
        PropertyChanged;

        private ICommand _clickCommand1;
        private ICommand _clickCommand2;
```

```
public string Name { get; set; }
public string Code { get; set; }

public ICommand ClickCommand_toname
{
    get
    {
        return _clickCommand1 ?? (_clickCommand1 = new
        CommandHandler(async () => {
            try
            {
                Name = await App.client.
                GetFromJsonAsync<string>("/encoder/
                codetoname?code=" + Code);
                PropertyChanged.Invoke(this, new
                PropertyChangedEventArgs("Name"));
            }
            catch (Exception ex)
            {
                MessageBox.Show(ex.Message);
            }
        }, () => CanExecute));
    }
}

public ICommand ClickCommand_tocode
{
    get
    {
        return _clickCommand2 ?? (_clickCommand2 = new
        CommandHandler(async () => {
```

```
            try
            {
                Code = await App.client.
                GetFromJsonAsync<string>("/encoder/
                nametocode?name=" + Name);
            PropertyChanged.Invoke(this, new
            PropertyChangedEventArgs("Code"));
            }
            catch (Exception ex)
            {
            MessageBox.Show(ex.Message);
            }
        }, () => CanExecute));
        }
    }
    public bool CanExecute
    {
        get
        {
            return true;
        }
    }

}
```

The next thing we need to look at is the encoder (See Listing 5-16). This in general is quite similar to what you saw previously, but we do have two commands instead of one. For that to work, you will also need two ICommand variables declared for the appropriate commands. With that, we avoid wasting space, and we execute all the logic inside the commands instead of having another method for it. Besides that, the arrangement is quite similar to the last feature; we use GetFromJsonAsync to make the conversion, and in case it fails, we use MessageBox to display the error.

Listing 5-17. XAML contents for the encoder view

```xml
<Grid>
        <TabControl>
            <TabItem Header="Code to name">
                <Grid Background="#FFE5E5E5">
                    <TextBox Text="{Binding Code}"
                    HorizontalAlignment="Left"
                    Margin="110,28,0,0" TextWrapping="Wrap"
                    VerticalAlignment="Top" Width="120"/>
                    <Label Content="Country code:"
                    HorizontalAlignment="Left"
                    Margin="10,24,0,0" VerticalAlignment="Top"
                    Width="95"/>
                    <Label Content="Country name:"
                    HorizontalAlignment="Left"
                    Margin="10,70,0,0" VerticalAlignment="Top"
                    Width="95"/>
                    <TextBox Text="{Binding Name,
                    Mode=OneWayToSource, UpdateSourceTrigger=
                    PropertyChanged}" IsReadOnly="True"
                    HorizontalAlignment="Left"
                    Margin="110,74,0,0" TextWrapping="Wrap"
                    VerticalAlignment="Top" Width="120"/>
                    <Button Command="{Binding
                    ClickCommand_toname}" Content="Submit"
                    HorizontalAlignment="Left"
                    Margin="110,109,0,0"
                    VerticalAlignment="Top" Width="120"/>
```

```
                </Grid>
            </TabItem>
            <TabItem Header="Name to code">
                <Grid Background="#FFE5E5E5">
                    <TextBox Text="{Binding Name}"
                    HorizontalAlignment="Left"
                    Margin="110,28,0,0" TextWrapping="Wrap"
                    VerticalAlignment="Top" Width="120"/>
                    <Label Content="Country name:"
                    HorizontalAlignment="Left"
                    Margin="10,24,0,0" VerticalAlignment="Top"
                    Width="95"/>
                    <Label Content="Country code:"
                    HorizontalAlignment="Left"
                    Margin="10,70,0,0" VerticalAlignment="Top"
                    Width="95"/>
                    <TextBox Text="{Binding Code,
                    Mode=TwoWay, UpdateSourceTrigger=P
                    ropertyChanged}" IsReadOnly="True"
                    HorizontalAlignment="Left"
                    Margin="110,74,0,0" TextWrapping="Wrap"
                    VerticalAlignment="Top" Width="120"/>
                    <Button Command="{Binding
                    ClickCommand_tocode}" Content="Submit"
                    HorizontalAlignment="Left"
                    Margin="110,109,0,0"
                    VerticalAlignment="Top" Width="120"/>
                </Grid>
            </TabItem>
        </TabControl>
</Grid>
```

Here (See Listing 5-17), we have the tab view arrangement; in it, we have four text boxes. But remember, we only have two variables. So, it is important how everything will be shared and that is why Tabs can be dangerous. In this case, we simply bind the appropriate text boxes to the properties in the ViewModel, and everything will work fine. With that, we only need to use two-way binding on the output boxes. Also, notice that the output text boxes are read-only; this allows the text to be copied and prohibits any other interactions. Finally, appropriate buttons have appropriate command, similar to declaring event for a specific button.

Listing 5-18. VerificationViewModel.cs

```
class VerificationViewModel
    {
        private ICommand _clickCommand;

        public SharedDataModels.CountryModel Country { get;
        set; } = new SharedDataModels.CountryModel();

        public ICommand ClickCommand_verify
        {
            get
            {
                return _clickCommand ?? (_clickCommand = new
                CommandHandler(async () => {
                    try
                    {
                        bool response = await (await App.
                        client.PostAsJsonAsync("/details/
                        verify", Country)).Content.
                        ReadFromJsonAsync<bool>();
```

```
                        if (response)
                        {
                            MessageBox.Show("Success");
                        }
                        else
                        {
                            MessageBox.Show("Failed");
                        }
                    }
                    catch (Exception ex)
                    {
                        MessageBox.Show(ex.Message);
                    }
                }, () => CanExecute));
            }
        }

        public bool CanExecute
        {
            get
            {
                return true;
            }
        }
    }
```

The final feature is a bit different in a sense that we are sending a body in the http request. To do that, we need to use PostAsJsonAsync and then access the Content property (See Listing 5-18). The Content property can be read as string, but we can also use ReadFromJsonAsync to get whatever type we want. Since the result is displayed in the message boxes, we do not need to notify about the property being changed.

Listing 5-19. XAML contents for the verification view

```
<Grid>
        <TextBox Text="{Binding Country.Country}"
        HorizontalAlignment="Left" Margin="86,121,0,0"
        TextWrapping="Wrap" VerticalAlignment="Top"
        Width="120"/>
        <TextBox Text="{Binding Country.Code}"
        HorizontalAlignment="Left" Margin="263,121,0,0"
        TextWrapping="Wrap" VerticalAlignment="Top"
        Width="120"/>
        <TextBox Text="{Binding Country.Domain}"
        HorizontalAlignment="Left" Margin="86,199,0,0"
        TextWrapping="Wrap" VerticalAlignment="Top"
        Width="120"/>
        <TextBox Text="{Binding Country.IsoCode}"
        HorizontalAlignment="Left" Margin="263,199,0,0"
        TextWrapping="Wrap" VerticalAlignment="Top"
        Width="120"/>
        <TextBox Text="{Binding Country.YearEstablished}"
        HorizontalAlignment="Left" Margin="178,276,0,0"
        TextWrapping="Wrap" VerticalAlignment="Top"
        Width="120"/>
        <Label Content="Country name"
        HorizontalAlignment="Left" Margin="86,95,0,0"
        VerticalAlignment="Top" Width="120"/>
        <Label Content="Country code"
        HorizontalAlignment="Left" Margin="263,95,0,0"
        VerticalAlignment="Top" Width="120"/>
        <Label Content="Domain" HorizontalAlignment="Left"
        Margin="86,173,0,0" VerticalAlignment="Top"
        Width="120"/>
```

```
<Label Content="ISO" HorizontalAlignment="Left"
Margin="263,173,0,0" VerticalAlignment="Top"
Width="120"/>
<Label Content="Year established"
HorizontalAlignment="Left" Margin="178,250,0,0"
VerticalAlignment="Top" Width="120"/>
<Button Content="Verify" Command="{Binding
ClickCommand_verify}" HorizontalAlignment="Left"
Margin="210,331,0,0" VerticalAlignment="Top"
Width="56"/>
```
```
</Grid>
```

Once again, after establishing the ViewModel, we need to bind everything to the controls in the XAML view (in this case, window) (See Listing 5-19). The button has command binding, but more importantly, each text box has bindings to properties of the model object. In this case, we do not use two-way binding anywhere, and with that, we do not have to state that or notify the UI, as mentioned previously.

Throughout this application, we have used exception messages to be displayed in case of an exception. This can be especially useful when tasking not in a debug mode, as your test users can reference specific exception instead of describing the issue in their own words.

Quick Exercise

Your task is to create a part of a simple local product management system. It will include product creation window and product lookup page.

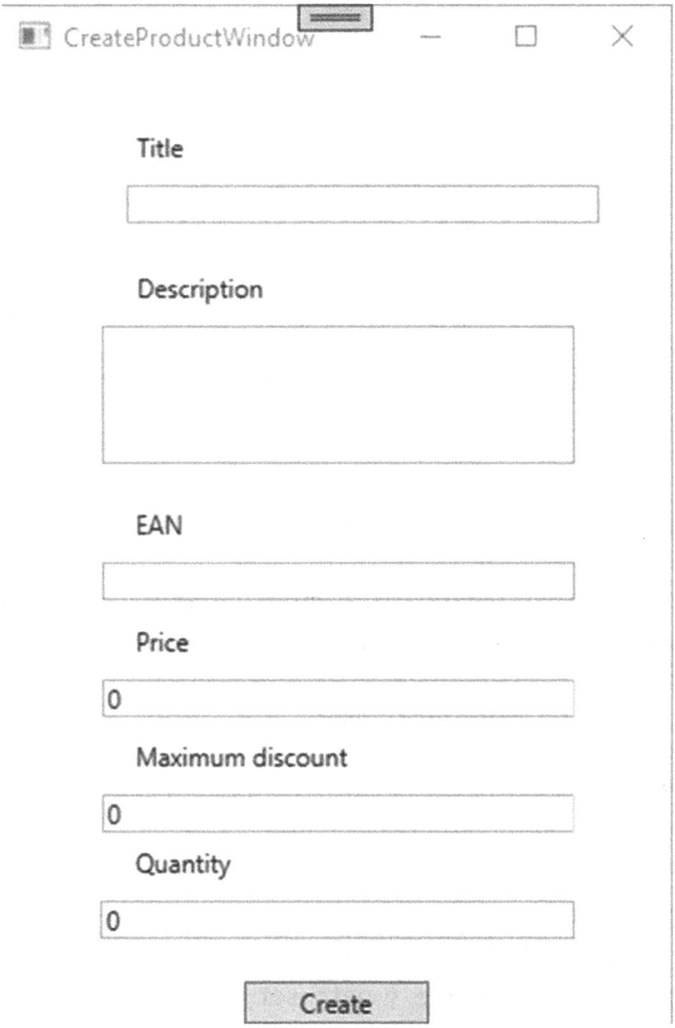

Figure 5-18. *Window for creating product*

The create product window should allow inputs as displayed in the image here (see Figure 5-18). Once created, a message box should be displayed and the values cleared.

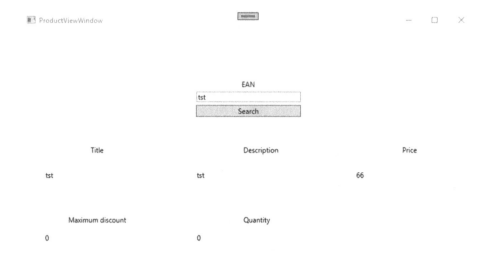

Figure 5-19. *Lookup window for the products*

Product lookup (see Figure 5-19) is quite simple as well; you should have a text box for EAN and display the result matching the value.

Listing 5-20. ProductHandler class

```
class ProductHandler
    {
        public class Product
        {
            public string EAN { get; set; }
            public int Price { get; set; }
            public int MaximumDiscount { get; set; }
            public string Title { get; set; }
            public string Description { get; set; }
            public double Quantity { get; set; }

        }
```

```csharp
public static async Task<List<Product>>
OpenProductsAsync()
{
    try
    {
        FileStream fl = File.OpenRead(Environment.
        GetFolderPath(Environment.SpecialFolder.
        ApplicationData) + "\\producthandler\\products.
        pmapp");
        byte[] bt = new byte[fl.Length];
        await fl.ReadAsync(bt);
        await fl.DisposeAsync();
        var data = JsonConvert.DeserializeObject<List
        <Product>>(System.Text.Encoding.UTF8.
        GetString(bt));
        return data;
    }
    catch (Exception e)
    {
        return null;
    }
}

public static async Task<bool>
WriteNewProductAsync(Product product)
{
    List<Product> current = new List<Product>();
    try
    {
        FileStream fl = File.Create(Environment.
        GetFolderPath(Environment.SpecialFolder.
        ApplicationData) + "\\producthandler\\products.
        pmapp");
```

```
                byte[] bt = new byte[fl.Length];
                await fl.ReadAsync(bt);
                await fl.DisposeAsync();
                if (bt.Length != 0)
                {
                    current = JsonConvert.DeserializeObject
                    <List<Product>>(System.Text.Encoding.UTF8.
                    GetString(bt));
                }
            }
            catch
            {
            }

            try
            {
                current.Add(product);
                FileStream flwrite = File.Create(Environment.
                GetFolderPath(Environment.SpecialFolder.
                ApplicationData) + "\\producthandler\\products.
                pmapp");
                flwrite.Write(System.Text.Encoding.
                UTF8.GetBytes(JsonConvert.
                SerializeObject(current)));
                return true;
            }
            catch (Exception e)
            {
                return false;
            }
        }
    }
```

To save the products and then look them up, you should use the provided class (see Listing 5-20). It also contains the model for the product data. WriteNewProductAsync takes a product object and writes that into the file. OpenProductsAsync will read the file and establish a list of products. Also, the directory provided does not exist right away, so you will need to use `System.IO.Directory.CreateDirectory` at some point.

Solution

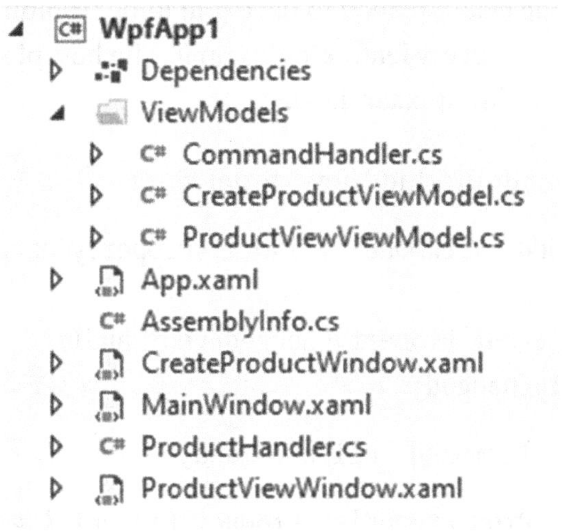

Figure 5-20.   *File layout for the solution example*

The file layout in the project (see Figure 5-20) is relatively straightforward. We have windows; we also have the ProductHandler class (see Listing 5-20). With that, we have ViewModels folder, similar to what you have seen in the "Quick Example" section. But in this case, we have a separate class file for the CommandHandler.

Listing 5-21. OnStartup event in App.xaml.cs

```
protected override void OnStartup(StartupEventArgs e)
        {
            System.IO.Directory.CreateDirectory(Environment.
            GetFolderPath(Environment.SpecialFolder.
            ApplicationData) + "\\producthandler");
            base.OnStartup(e);
        }
```

Before anything else, we need to have that folder established (See Listing 5-21), because every feature relies on it. The best place to do it is in the OnStartup event (in App.xaml.cs).

Listing 5-22. CreateProductViewModel.cs

```
class CreateProductViewModel : INotifyPropertyChanged
    {
        public event PropertyChangedEventHandler
        PropertyChanged;

        private ICommand _clickCommand;

        public  ProductHandler.Product Product { get; set; } =
        new ProductHandler.Product();

        public ICommand ClickCommand
        {
            get
            {
                return _clickCommand ?? (_clickCommand = new
                CommandHandler(async () => {
                    if (await ProductHandler.
                    WriteNewProductAsync(Product)){
                        MessageBox.Show("Product added");
```

```
            Product = new ProductHandler.Product();
            PropertyChanged.Invoke(this, new
            PropertyChangedEventArgs("Product"));
        }
        else
        {
            MessageBox.Show("Something went
            wrong");
        }
    }, () => CanExecute));
    }
}
public bool CanExecute
{
    get
    {
        return true;
    }
}
}
```

We can begin with CreateProductViewModel (See Listing 5-22), which will be associated with CreateProductWindow. This is similar to what you saw before; we have PropertyChangedEventHandler, we have ICommand implemented, and we have our property declared. Remember, for this to work, the property (in this case, Product) must be public; this mistake, as mentioned previously, is easy to make and difficult to find. Besides all the fancy MVVM stuff, we simply execute WriteNewProductAsync and check for the Boolean value to be true; if it is, we reset the product values for new input.

Listing 5-23. XAML code for the create product view

```
<Grid>
        <Button Content="Create" Command="{Binding
        ClickCommand}" HorizontalAlignment="Center"
        Margin="0,428,0,0" VerticalAlignment="Top" Width="88"/>
        <Label Content="Title" HorizontalAlignment="Left"
        Margin="59,23,0,0" VerticalAlignment="Top"
        Width="171"/>
        <TextBox Text="{Binding Product.Title, Mode=TwoWay,
        UpdateSourceTrigger=PropertyChanged}"
        HorizontalAlignment="Left" Margin="59,54,0,0"
        TextWrapping="Wrap" VerticalAlignment="Top"
        Width="225"/>
        <Label Content="Description" HorizontalAlignment="Left"
        Margin="59,89,0,0" VerticalAlignment="Top"
        Width="171"/>
        <TextBox Text="{Binding Product.Description,
        Mode=TwoWay, UpdateSourceTrigger=PropertyChanged}"
        HorizontalAlignment="Center" Margin="0,120,0,0"
        TextWrapping="Wrap" VerticalAlignment="Top" Width="225"
        Height="65"/>
        <Label Content="EAN" HorizontalAlignment="Left"
        Margin="58,200,0,0" VerticalAlignment="Top"
        Width="171"/>
        <TextBox Text="{Binding Product.EAN, Mode=TwoWay,
        UpdateSourceTrigger=PropertyChanged}"
        HorizontalAlignment="Center" Margin="0,231,0,0"
        TextWrapping="Wrap" VerticalAlignment="Top"
        Width="225"/>
```

```
<Label Content="Price" HorizontalAlignment="Left"
Margin="58,255,0,0" VerticalAlignment="Top"
Width="171"/>
<TextBox Text="{Binding Product.Price, Mode=TwoWay,
UpdateSourceTrigger=PropertyChanged}"
HorizontalAlignment="Center" Margin="0,286,0,0"
TextWrapping="Wrap" VerticalAlignment="Top"
Width="225"/>
<Label Content="Maximum discount"
HorizontalAlignment="Left" Margin="58,309,0,0"
VerticalAlignment="Top" Width="171"/>
<TextBox Text="{Binding Product.MaximumDiscount,
Mode=TwoWay, UpdateSourceTrigger=PropertyChanged}"
HorizontalAlignment="Center" Margin="0,340,0,0"
TextWrapping="Wrap" VerticalAlignment="Top"
Width="225"/>
<Label Content="Quantity" HorizontalAlignment="Left"
Margin="58,359,0,0" VerticalAlignment="Top"
Width="171"/>
<TextBox Text="{Binding Product.Quantity,
Mode=TwoWay, UpdateSourceTrigger=PropertyChanged}"
HorizontalAlignment="Center" Margin="0,390,0,0"
TextWrapping="Wrap" VerticalAlignment="Top"
Width="226"/>
</Grid>
```

In the XAML (See Listing 5-23), we bind the properties of Product using two-way binding. Remember, we do set the values to insert the product, but then we also reset the values and that is why we need two-way binding in this case.

Listing 5-24. ProductViewModel.cs

```
class ProductViewViewModel : INotifyPropertyChanged
    {
        public event PropertyChangedEventHandler
        PropertyChanged;

        private ICommand _clickCommand;

        public  List<ProductHandler.Product> Products { get;
        set; }
        public ProductHandler.Product DisplayedProduct { get;
        set; } = new ProductHandler.Product();

        public ICommand ClickCommand
        {
            get
            {
                return _clickCommand ?? (_clickCommand = new
                CommandHandler(async () => {
                    try
                    {
if (Products == null)
                        {
                            Products = await ProductHandler.
                            OpenProductsAsync();
                        }
                        DisplayedProduct = Products.Find(p =>
                        p.EAN == DisplayedProduct.EAN);
                        PropertyChanged.Invoke(this, new
                        PropertyChangedEventArgs("
                        DisplayedProduct"));
                    }
```

```
                catch (Exception e)
                {
                    MessageBox.Show(e.Message);
                }
            }, () => CanExecute));
        }
    }
    public bool CanExecute
    {
        get
        {
            return true;
        }
    }
}
```

The lookup feature is a bit more complex, but it still retains the basic arrangement of the ViewModel (See Listing 5-24). In this case, we need to retrieve the list of products from that file, but there is no good reason to read it and hold it in the memory on the start of the application. What we do here is read it and assign it to a list variable only when the search has been initiated. We only retrieve it once by checking if the variable is null; if not, we skip this step. Such arrangements may save time and resources, but do always be careful as this is essentially a form of caching and that can lead to missed updates and similar issues. Besides that, we simply use Find to retrieve the record with matching EAN from the list.

Listing 5-25. XAML code for the lookup view

```
<Grid>
        <TextBox Text="{Binding DisplayedProduct.EAN,
        Mode=TwoWay, UpdateSourceTrigger=PropertyChanged}"
        HorizontalAlignment="Center" Margin="0,106,0,0"
        TextWrapping="Wrap" VerticalAlignment="Top"
        Width="179"/>
        <Label Content="EAN" HorizontalAlignment="Center"
        Margin="0,80,0,0" VerticalAlignment="Top"/>
        <Button Command="{Binding ClickCommand}"
        Content="Search" HorizontalAlignment="Center"
        Margin="0,129,0,0" VerticalAlignment="Top"
        Width="180"/>
        <Label Content="Title" HorizontalAlignment="Left"
        Margin="113,0,0,0" VerticalAlignment="Center"/>
        <Label Content="{Binding DisplayedProduct.Title,
        Mode=TwoWay, UpdateSourceTrigger=PropertyChanged}"
        HorizontalAlignment="Left" Margin="34,235,0,0"
        VerticalAlignment="Top" Width="191"/>
        <Label Content="Description" HorizontalAlignment="Left"
        Margin="378,0,0,0" VerticalAlignment="Center"/>
        <Label Content="{Binding DisplayedProduct.Description,
        Mode=TwoWay, UpdateSourceTrigger=PropertyChanged}"
        HorizontalAlignment="Left" Margin="298,235,0,0"
        VerticalAlignment="Top" Width="192"/>
        <Label Content="Price" HorizontalAlignment="Left"
        Margin="653,0,0,0" VerticalAlignment="Center"/>
        <Label Content="{Binding DisplayedProduct.Price,
        Mode=TwoWay, UpdateSourceTrigger=PropertyChanged}"
        HorizontalAlignment="Left" Margin="573,235,0,0"
        VerticalAlignment="Top" Width="192"/>
```

```
<Label Content="Maximum discount"
HorizontalAlignment="Left" Margin="73,311,0,0"
VerticalAlignment="Top"/>
<Label Content="{Binding DisplayedProduct.
MaximumDiscount, Mode=TwoWay, UpdateSourceTrigger=
PropertyChanged}" HorizontalAlignment="Left"
Margin="33,342,0,0" VerticalAlignment="Top"
Width="192"/>
<Label Content="Quantity" HorizontalAlignment="Left"
Margin="378,311,0,0" VerticalAlignment="Top"/>
<Label Content="{Binding DisplayedProduct.Quantity,
Mode=TwoWay, UpdateSourceTrigger=PropertyChanged}"
HorizontalAlignment="Left" Margin="298,342,0,0"
VerticalAlignment="Top" Width="192"/>
</Grid>
```

Finally, we have the XAML code (See Listing 5-25) where we have our elements laid out and bindings set. This is similar to what you have seen many times; we begin with setting up the logic in the ViewModel and then bind the data to the UI elements in the XAML.

CHAPTER 6

Styles

In the previous chapters, you have seen some design properties being set and adjusted. In this chapter, you will learn how to add some additional ones, how to deal with some window design elements, and how to create style templates.

Window Size and Other Sizes

If you read the previous chapters of the book, you already know how to set up the elements, change properties, and use them in other ways. However, in most cases, you will need to make some adjustments to the window and perhaps make some other arrangements to fit everything in your window. We will first look at four different arrangements in terms of window, and then we will look at something called stack panel.

© Taurius Litvinavicius 2021
T. Litvinavicius, *Exploring Windows Presentation Foundation*,
https://doi.org/10.1007/978-1-4842-6637-3_6

Figure 6-1. *File layout for the example project*

In this example, we have four new windows added, alongside the main window (see Figure 6-1).

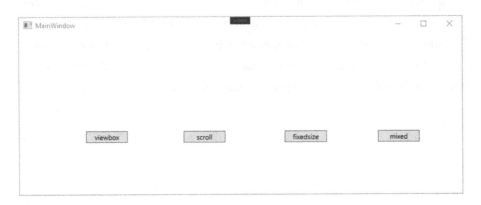

Figure 6-2. *MainWindow layout for the example*

The main window has four buttons (see Figure 6-2), which when clicked will open each example window.

Figure 6-3. *First state of the view box example*

Figure 6-4. *First state of the view box example*

Listing 6-1. XAML code for the view box example

```
<Window x:Class="WpfApp17.viewboxwindow"
        xmlns="http://schemas.microsoft.com/winfx/2006/xaml/
        presentation"
        xmlns:x="http://schemas.microsoft.com/winfx/2006/xaml"
```

```
    xmlns:d="http://schemas.microsoft.com/expression/
    blend/2008"
    xmlns:mc="http://schemas.openxmlformats.org/markup-
    compatibility/2006"
    xmlns:local="clr-namespace:WpfApp17"
    mc:Ignorable="d"
    Title="viewboxwindow" Height="450" MinHeight="200"
    MinWidth="300" Width="800">
<Viewbox Margin="0,0,0,0" >
    <Grid Margin="0,0,0,0" >
        <TextBlock Margin="0,0,5,5">text  1</TextBlock>
    </Grid>
</Viewbox>
</Window>
```

The first example uses a ViewBox to resize the content automatically
(See Listing 6-1) and always make it fit to the window. As you can see,
the first image (Figure 6-3) is regular window size, and the second one
(Figure 6-4) is the same image resized to a smaller size. The text has shrunk
along with the window size, but this arrangement should be used with
caution. The best thing to do is always use MinHeight and MinWidth with
the ViewBox. The ViewBox itself must wrap a Grid element; you may also
have additional grid inside the main grid and wrap that one.

Figure 6-5. *Scroll viewer example view*

The next option is the scroll arrangement (see Figure 6-5), a more traditional one, but it is usually the easiest one to implement.

Listing 6-2. XAML listing for scroll viewer example

```
<Window x:Class="WpfApp17.scrollwindow"
        xmlns="http://schemas.microsoft.com/winfx/2006/xaml/
        presentation"
        xmlns:x="http://schemas.microsoft.com/winfx/2006/xaml"
        xmlns:d="http://schemas.microsoft.com/expression/
        blend/2008"
        xmlns:mc="http://schemas.openxmlformats.org/markup-
        compatibility/2006"
        xmlns:local="clr-namespace:WpfApp17"
        mc:Ignorable="d"
        Title="scrollwindow" Height="450" Width="800">
```

```
<ScrollViewer HorizontalScrollBarVisibility="Auto" >
    <Grid  Height="800" Margin="0,0,0,0" Width="955">
        <Button Content="Button"
        HorizontalAlignment="Left" Margin="90,500,0,0"
        VerticalAlignment="Top" Width="76"/>
        <Button Content="Button" HorizontalAlignment="Left"
        Margin="800,261,0,0" VerticalAlignment="Top"
        Width="75"/>
    </Grid>
</ScrollViewer>
</Window>
```

ScrollViewer (See Listing 6-2 amd Figure 6-5) allows the content to overflow, and you need to wrap your containers (e.g., Grid) with it. The process is very similar to the ViewBox, but there are some additional things to remember here. You can see the scroll bar visibility by setting either HorizontalScrollBarVisibility or HorizontalScrollBarVisibility or both.

Another thing you can do is simply set your window to a fixed size. This is a great option, but you must make sure that the window size is small enough to fit most devices.

Listing 6-3. XAML code for window resize options example

```
<Window x:Class="WpfApp17.fixedsizewindow"
        xmlns="http://schemas.microsoft.com/winfx/2006/xaml/
        presentation"
        xmlns:x="http://schemas.microsoft.com/winfx/2006/xaml"
        xmlns:d="http://schemas.microsoft.com/expression/
        blend/2008"
        xmlns:mc="http://schemas.openxmlformats.org/markup-
        compatibility/2006"
```

```
        xmlns:local="clr-namespace:WpfApp17"
        mc:Ignorable="d"
        ResizeMode="NoResize"
        Title="fixedsizewindow" Height="450" Width="800">
    <Grid></Grid>
</Window>
```

If you want to have it fixed, you simply need to set ResizeMode to NoResize (See Listing 6-3). However, this option also does not allow the window to minimize. So, if you wish to have the ability to minimize but no ability to resize, you need to set ResizeMode to CanMinimize.

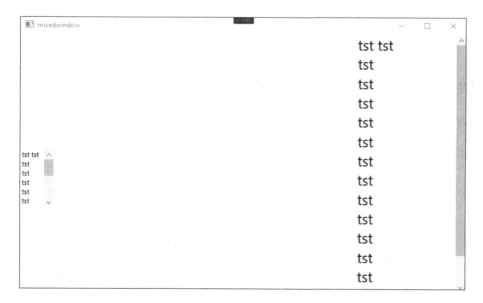

Figure 6-6. *View for the mixed example*

Figure 6-7. *Second state of the mixed example*

Listing 6-4. XAML code for the mixed example

```
<Window x:Class="WpfApp17.mixedwindow"
        xmlns="http://schemas.microsoft.com/winfx/2006/xaml/
        presentation"
        xmlns:x="http://schemas.microsoft.com/winfx/2006/xaml"
        xmlns:d="http://schemas.microsoft.com/expression/
        blend/2008"
        xmlns:mc="http://schemas.openxmlformats.org/markup-
        compatibility/2006"
        xmlns:local="clr-namespace:WpfApp17"
        mc:Ignorable="d"
        Title="mixedwindow" Height="450" Width="800">
    <ScrollViewer>
    <Grid>
```

```
<ScrollViewer HorizontalAlignment="Left" Width="56"
Height="100">
<TextBlock HorizontalAlignment="Left" Margin="0,0,0,0"
TextWrapping="Wrap" VerticalAlignment="Top"
Height="auto" Width="56"><Run Text="tst tst
"/><LineBreak/><Run Text="tst "/><LineBreak/><Run
Text="tst "/><LineBreak/><Run Text="tst
"/><LineBreak/><Run Text="tst "/><LineBreak/><Run
Text="tst "/><LineBreak/><Run Text="tst
"/><LineBreak/><Run Text="tst "/><LineBreak/><Run
Text="tst "/><LineBreak/><Run Text="tst
"/><LineBreak/><Run Text="tst "/><LineBreak/><Run
Text="tst "/><LineBreak/><Run Text="tst
"/><LineBreak/><Run Text="tst "/><LineBreak/><Run/></
TextBlock>
</ScrollViewer>
<Viewbox Margin="536,0,0,0" MinHeight="300"
MaxHeight="500">
<Grid HorizontalAlignment="Left"   Margin="0,0,0,0">
    <TextBlock HorizontalAlignment="Left"
    Margin="0,0,0,0" TextWrapping="Wrap"
    VerticalAlignment="Top" Height="auto"
    Width="56"><Run Text="tst tst "/><LineBreak/><Run
    Text="tst "/><LineBreak/><Run Text="tst
    "/><LineBreak/><Run Text="tst "/><LineBreak/><Run
    Text="tst "/><LineBreak/><Run Text="tst
    "/><LineBreak/><Run Text="tst "/><LineBreak/><Run
    Text="tst "/><LineBreak/><Run Text="tst
    "/><LineBreak/><Run Text="tst "/><LineBreak/><Run
    Text="tst "/><LineBreak/><Run Text="tst
    "/><LineBreak/><Run Text="tst "/><LineBreak/><Run
    Text="tst "/><LineBreak/><Run/></TextBlock>
```

```
            </Grid>
        </Viewbox>
    </Grid>
    </ScrollViewer>
</Window>
```

The whole grid in this example is in a scroll viewer (See Listing 6-4). But with that, we also have overflowing elements in the TextBlock which is wrapped in a scroll viewer. This TextBlock is not relative in any way to the window, so if the window size changes (compare Figures 6-6 and 6-7), the TextBlock will stay the same. On the other hand, we have another TextBlock, which is wrapped in a ViewBox, and that arrangement is relative to the window size. If it changes, the size of the TextBlock will change as well.

Style

Throughout this book, you have already seen some style properties being set in XAML for each element and in C#. In this section, we will explore this further, and you will also learn how to create a style arrangement and apply one setup for several elements of the same type.

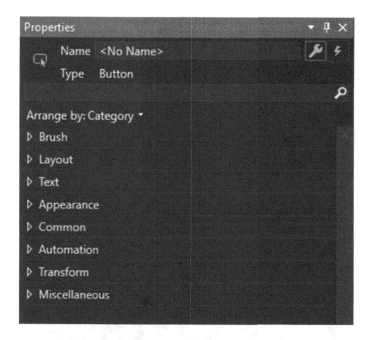

Figure 6-8. *Properties section in visual studio*

You have already seen this before in this book and highly likely in visual studio as well. Whenever you select an element in XAML, you will be able to access its properties in the properties window (see Figure 6-8). You can set all of them in XAML, but this is an easier way to do it, especially with color values. You can also set events through this arrangement.

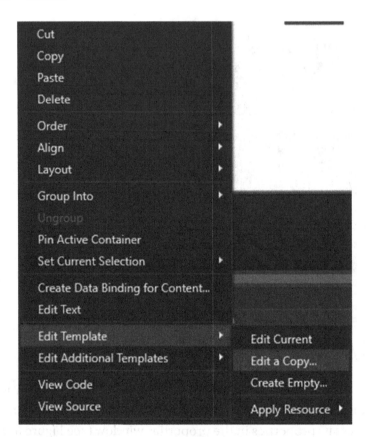

Figure 6-9. *"Edit a Copy..." selection in visual studio*

The style properties can be set to each element specifically (See Figure 6-8), but you can also create a style template and apply to several elements. This can be extremely useful when doing complicated design on a project that has lots of elements. The element style templates are created for specific element types (e.g., buttons), and to establish one, you need to right-click the element in the XAML editor (not the XAML code), then go to "Edit Template", and then choose "Edit a Copy..." (see Figure 6-9). You could create an empty template, but that is usually a waste of time and requires a lot more knowledge, and focus to actually make everything work. If you go with the copy, the defaults of the element will be applied, and then you will simply be able to change colors, sizes, and other properties.

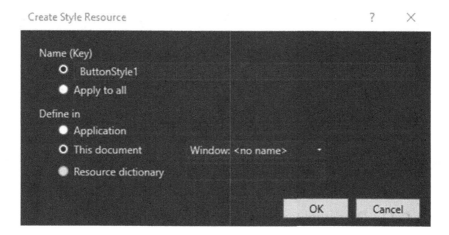

Figure 6-10. *Template setup in visual studio*

Once you click "Edit a Copy..." (See Figure 6-9), another window will open (see Figure 6-10). This one is very important, as this is where you choose where you want the style template code to be saved. For that, you have three options: Application will save it in the App.xaml code file, This document will place the code in the current window, and Resource dictionary will save the code in a separate file, but we will look at that arrangement later. You also have to choose between setting a key for the style and applying it to all elements of that type. You should always go with the key and apply it separately, even if you do intend to apply it to all. That will help if you need to make changes to the code later.

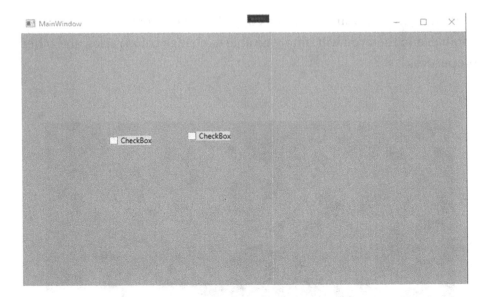

Figure 6-11. *First state for the example*

Figure 6-12. *Second state for the example*

We will now look at an example of the implementation of these templates. The window here (see Figures 6-11 and 6-12) has an orange background, the check boxes have light blue background, and the check mark on the box is custom.

Listing 6-5. XAML code for the window style template (in App.xaml file)

```
<Application.Resources>

        <ControlTemplate x:Key="WindowTemplateKey"
        TargetType="{x:Type Window}">
```

```
<Border BorderBrush="{TemplateBinding BorderBrush}"
BorderThickness="{TemplateBinding BorderThickness}"
Background="{TemplateBinding Background}">
    <Grid>
        <AdornerDecorator>
            <ContentPresenter/>
        </AdornerDecorator>
        <ResizeGrip x:Name="WindowResizeGrip"
        HorizontalAlignment="Right"
        IsTabStop="false" Visibility="Collapsed"
        VerticalAlignment="Bottom"/>
    </Grid>
</Border>
<ControlTemplate.Triggers>
    <MultiTrigger>
        <MultiTrigger.Conditions>
            <Condition Property="ResizeMode"
            Value="CanResizeWithGrip"/>
            <Condition Property="WindowState"
            Value="Normal"/>
        </MultiTrigger.Conditions>
        <Setter Property="Visibility"
        TargetName="WindowResizeGrip"
        Value="Visible"/>
    </MultiTrigger>
</ControlTemplate.Triggers>
</ControlTemplate>
<Style x:Key="WindowStyle1" TargetType="{x:Type Window}">
    <Setter Property="Foreground"
    Value="{DynamicResource {x:Static SystemColors.
    WindowTextBrushKey}}"/>
```

```
            <Setter Property="Background" Value="Orange"/>
            <Setter Property="Template">
                <Setter.Value>
                    <ControlTemplate TargetType="{x:Type
                    Window}">
                        <Border BorderBrush="{TemplateBinding
                        BorderBrush}" BorderThickness="{T
                        emplateBinding BorderThickness}"
                        Background="{TemplateBinding
                        Background}">
                            <AdornerDecorator>
                                <ContentPresenter/>
                            </AdornerDecorator>
                        </Border>
                    </ControlTemplate>
                </Setter.Value>
            </Setter>
            <Style.Triggers>
                <Trigger Property="ResizeMode"
                Value="CanResizeWithGrip">
                    <Setter Property="Template"
                    Value="{StaticResource
                    WindowTemplateKey}"/>
                </Trigger>
            </Style.Triggers>
        </Style>
</Application.Resources>
```

The window template was created as an application (App.xaml).
Although you do not drag and drop the Window, it is still an element of
WPF, and it can have style templates just like any other. When you create
one of these style arrangements, you get a lot of XAML code, but it is

important to understand what you can modify and what is just a noise and should be left alone. First in the code, you have ControlTemplate; it may seem like something important, but actually, it should all be left alone. After the ControlTemplate, we have Style, and this is what really matters. You can see that we have Key and TargetType; they will be used to reference a style template in the element, and that is how you apply the template to an element. The type simply states which type of element this is for. Inside there, we have something called Setter – it can be simple or very complex. Setter helps you set values for properties; you can simply declare the property in Property (e.g., Background) and then Value (in this case, Orange color). You may also notice the Property Template, which is set in a more complex way and should not be changed, but you can see how the value can be more complex here. Another important part is the Style.Triggers; this one is very important, and you will see more about it when we look at the check box style. But basically, Triggers describe what things should look like on certain events (e.g., GotFocus).

Listing 6-6. Window element in MainWindow.xaml

```
<Window x:Class="WpfApp30.MainWindow"
        xmlns="http://schemas.microsoft.com/winfx/2006/xaml/
        presentation"
        xmlns:x="http://schemas.microsoft.com/winfx/2006/xaml"
        xmlns:d="http://schemas.microsoft.com/expression/
        blend/2008"
        xmlns:mc="http://schemas.openxmlformats.org/markup-
        compatibility/2006"
        xmlns:local="clr-namespace:WpfApp30"
        mc:Ignorable="d"

        Title="MainWindow" Height="450" Width="800"
        Style="{DynamicResource WindowStyle1}">
```

Our main window has a style template (See Listing 6-6). The way
it is set is quite simple – you need to declare the Style property and use
DynamicResource, as shown in the example. DynamicResource is the key
of the template, and it will be declared the same way from the application
as it would be from the window.

Listing 6-7. Resources in window

```
<Window.Resources>
        <Style x:Key="FocusVisual">
            <Setter Property="Control.Template">
                <Setter.Value>
                    <ControlTemplate>
                        <Rectangle Margin="2"
                        SnapsToDevicePixels="true"
                        Stroke="{DynamicResource {x:Static
                        SystemColors.ControlTextBrushKey}}"
                        StrokeThickness="1" StrokeDashArray="1
                        2"/>
                    </ControlTemplate>
                </Setter.Value>
            </Setter>
        </Style>
        <SolidColorBrush x:Key="OptionMark.Static.Background"
        Color="#FFFFFFFF"/>
        <SolidColorBrush x:Key="OptionMark.Static.Border"
        Color="#FF707070"/>
        <Style x:Key="OptionMarkFocusVisual">
            <Setter Property="Control.Template">
                <Setter.Value>
                    <ControlTemplate>
```

```
                    <Rectangle Margin="14,0,0,0"
                    SnapsToDevicePixels="true"
                    Stroke="{DynamicResource {x:Static
                    SystemColors.ControlTextBrushKey}}"
                    StrokeThickness="1" StrokeDashArray="1
                    2"/>
                </ControlTemplate>
            </Setter.Value>
        </Setter>
    </Style>
    <SolidColorBrush x:Key="OptionMark.MouseOver.
    Background" Color="#FFF3F9FF"/>
    <SolidColorBrush x:Key="OptionMark.MouseOver.Border"
    Color="#FF5593FF"/>
    <SolidColorBrush x:Key="OptionMark.MouseOver.Glyph"
    Color="#FF212121"/>
    <SolidColorBrush x:Key="OptionMark.Disabled.Background"
    Color="#FFE6E6E6"/>
    <SolidColorBrush x:Key="OptionMark.Disabled.Border"
    Color="#FFBCBCBC"/>
    <SolidColorBrush x:Key="OptionMark.Disabled.Glyph"
    Color="#FF707070"/>
    <SolidColorBrush x:Key="OptionMark.Pressed.Background"
    Color="#FFD9ECFF"/>
    <SolidColorBrush x:Key="OptionMark.Pressed.Border"
    Color="#FF3C77DD"/>
    <SolidColorBrush x:Key="OptionMark.Pressed.Glyph"
    Color="#FF212121"/>
    <SolidColorBrush x:Key="OptionMark.Static.Glyph"
    Color="#FF212121"/>
```

169

```xml
<Style x:Key="CheckBoxStyle" TargetType="{x:Type
CheckBox}">
    <Setter Property="FocusVisualStyle"
    Value="{StaticResource FocusVisual}"/>
    <Setter Property="Background" Value="FloralWhite"/>
    <Setter Property="BorderBrush"
    Value="{StaticResource OptionMark.Static.Border}"/>
    <Setter Property="Foreground"
    Value="{DynamicResource {x:Static SystemColors.
    ControlTextBrushKey}}"/>
    <Setter Property="BorderThickness" Value="1"/>
    <Setter Property="Template">
        <Setter.Value>
            <ControlTemplate TargetType="{x:Type
            CheckBox}">
                <Grid x:Name="templateRoot"
                Background="Aqua"
                SnapsToDevicePixels="True">
                    <Grid.ColumnDefinitions>
                        <ColumnDefinition
                        Width="Auto"/>
                        <ColumnDefinition Width="*"/>
                    </Grid.ColumnDefinitions>
                    <Border x:Name="checkBoxBorder"
                    BorderBrush="HotPink" BorderThickness
                    ="{TemplateBinding BorderThickness}"
                    Background="{TemplateBinding
                    Background}" HorizontalAl
                    ignment="{TemplateBinding
                    HorizontalContentAlignment}"
                    Margin="1" VerticalAlignment="{Templa
                    teBinding VerticalContentAlignment}">
```

```xml
<Grid x:Name="markGrid">
    <Path x:Name="optionMark"
    Data="F1 M 9.97498,1.22334L
    4.6983,9.09834L
    4.52164,9.09834L 0,5.19331L
    1.27664,3.52165L
    4.255,6.08833L
    2.33331,1.52588e-005L
    2.97498,1.22334 Z "
    Fill="{StaticResource
    OptionMark.Static.Glyph}"
    Margin="1" Opacity="0"
    Stretch="None"/>
    <Rectangle
    x:Name="indeterminateMark"
    Fill="{StaticResource
    OptionMark.Static.Glyph}"
    Margin="2" Opacity="0"/>
</Grid>
</Border>
<ContentPresenter
x:Name="contentPresenter" Grid.
Column="1" Focusable="False" Hor
izontalAlignment="{TemplateBindi
ng HorizontalContentAlignment}"
Margin="{TemplateBinding Padding}"
RecognizesAccessKey="True" Snap
sToDevicePixels="{TemplateBindi
ng SnapsToDevicePixels}" Verti
calAlignment="{TemplateBinding
VerticalContentAlignment}"/>
</Grid>
```

```
<ControlTemplate.Triggers>
    <Trigger Property="HasContent"
    Value="true">
        <Setter
        Property="FocusVisualStyle"
        Value="{StaticResource
        OptionMarkFocusVisual}"/>
        <Setter Property="Padding"
        Value="4,-1,0,0"/>
    </Trigger>
    <Trigger Property="IsMouseOver"
    Value="true">
        <Setter Property="Background"
        TargetName="checkBoxBorder"
        Value="{StaticResource
        OptionMark.MouseOver.
        Background}"/>
        <Setter Property="BorderBrush"
        TargetName="checkBoxBorder"
        Value="{StaticResource
        OptionMark.MouseOver.Border}"/>
        <Setter Property="Fill"
        TargetName="optionMark"
        Value="{StaticResource
        OptionMark.MouseOver.Glyph}"/>
        <Setter Property="Fill"
        TargetName="indeterminateMark"
        Value="{StaticResource
        OptionMark.MouseOver.Glyph}"/>
    </Trigger>
    <Trigger Property="IsEnabled"
    Value="false">
```

```
    <Setter Property="Background"
    TargetName="checkBoxBorder"
    Value="{StaticResource
    OptionMark.Disabled.
    Background}"/>
    <Setter Property="BorderBrush"
    TargetName="checkBoxBorder"
    Value="{StaticResource
    OptionMark.Disabled.Border}"/>
    <Setter Property="Fill"
    TargetName="optionMark"
    Value="{StaticResource
    OptionMark.Disabled.Glyph}"/>
    <Setter Property="Fill"
    TargetName="indeterminateMark"
    Value="{StaticResource
    OptionMark.Disabled.Glyph}"/>
</Trigger>
<Trigger Property="IsPressed"
Value="true">
    <Setter Property="Background"
    TargetName="checkBoxBorder"
    Value="{StaticResource
    OptionMark.Pressed.Background}"/>
    <Setter Property="BorderBrush"
    TargetName="checkBoxBorder"
    Value="{StaticResource
    OptionMark.Pressed.Border}"/>
    <Setter Property="Fill"
    TargetName="optionMark"
    Value="{StaticResource
    OptionMark.Pressed.Glyph}"/>
```

173

```xml
                            <Setter Property="Fill"
                            TargetName="indeterminateMark"
                            Value="{StaticResource
                            OptionMark.Pressed.Glyph}"/>
                        </Trigger>
                        <Trigger Property="IsChecked"
                        Value="true">
                            <Setter Property="Opacity"
                            TargetName="optionMark"
                            Value="1"/>
                            <Setter Property="Opacity"
                            TargetName="indeterminateMark"
                            Value="0"/>
                        </Trigger>
                        <Trigger Property="IsChecked"
                        Value="{x:Null}">
                            <Setter Property="Opacity"
                            TargetName="optionMark"
                            Value="0"/>
                            <Setter Property="Opacity"
                            TargetName="indeterminateMark"
                            Value="1"/>
                        </Trigger>
                    </ControlTemplate.Triggers>
                </ControlTemplate>
            </Setter.Value>
        </Setter>
    </Style>
</Window.Resources>
```

The code (See Listing 6-7) for the check boxes is more complex, but once again you should only deal with what matters here. Remember, when you set the style template for the element, you use a key value to do it. So, to find what matters, you need to find the part where that key is stated. If you look here, you should ignore everything from the top of the code to the Style element with x:Key="CheckBoxStyle" declared. In this case, you can see that we have the background changed from the default value. The most interesting thing here is the check mark for the box. You can find that in the Grid (named markGrid); this is the little box you see on the left of the whole arrangement. The mark itself is the Path, named optionMark, where we have Fill and Data as two most important properties. The Data part may seem a bit strange, but simply sets various points of the shape that will be drawn.

When dealing with style templates for any element, you must always look for what you really need to change and avoid any changes to what will stay default.

At this point, you know how to create style template in both Window and App.xaml files. You also know what to look for and what to avoid. There is one more thing you have to know; that is how to create these templates in a separate file.

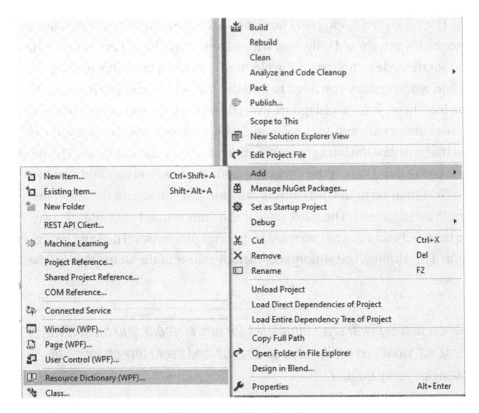

Figure 6-13. *Resource dictionary file selection*

To place your templates in a dictionary, you first need to create a dictionary (see Figure 6-13). It is a simple .xaml file, with some basic content in it. But before you can edit a copy, you still need to do something else.

Listing 6-8. Resource dictionary reference in window

```
<Window.Resources>
        <ResourceDictionary>
            <ResourceDictionary.MergedDictionaries>
                <ResourceDictionary Source="Dictionary1.xaml"/>
            </ResourceDictionary.MergedDictionaries>
        </ResourceDictionary>
</Window.Resources>
```

In the Window (in which you will use the template), you need to reference the dictionary file as stated in the example. You can add several of them by adding more ResourceDictionary statements (See Listing 6-8).

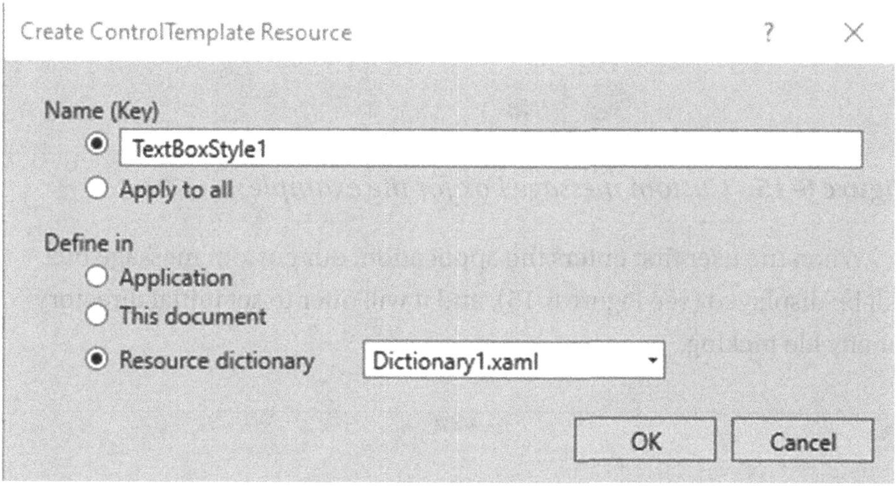

Figure 6-14. *Creating style template in resource dictionary*

Finally, once you do all that, you select your element and create new template as a copy. If you reference more than one dictionary file, you can select them at this point.

Quick Example

For this example, you will see a file verification application. It allows the user to create a signature for a file, which is then saved locally and can be verified later.

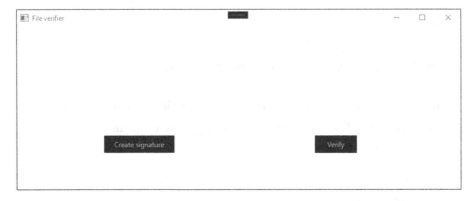

Figure 6-15. *Custom message box for the example*

When the user first enters the application, our custom message box will be displayed (see Figure 6-15), and it will offer to set initial directory for any file picking.

Figure 6-16. *Main window for the example*

Once the first step is taken, the user will be able to either create a signature or verify a file against the saved data (see Figure 6-16).

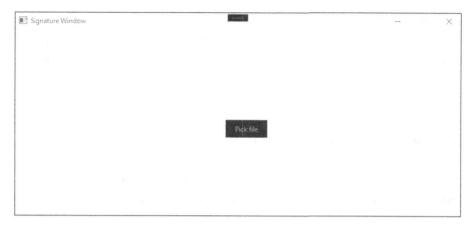

Figure 6-17. *Initial view for the signature creation window*

If the user chooses to create new signature, they will see a new window
(see Figure 6-17) with a button which when clicked will display a file picker
window.

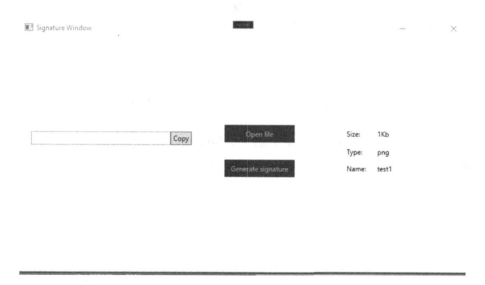

Figure 6-18. *Signature creation window after the file is selected*

179

Once the file is picked, the user will see the size, the type, and the file name (see Figure 6-18). The signature will only be created once the "Generate signature" button is clicked. The user may also open the file.

Figure 6-19. *Signature displayed in the text box*

Once the signature is generated, it will be displayed in the box (see Figure 6-19). The copy button will copy the value to the clipboard.

Figure 6-20. *Initial view for file verification window*

If the user chooses to verify, they will first have to pick a file for verifications (see Figure 6-20).

Figure 6-21. *Text displayed when file is valid*

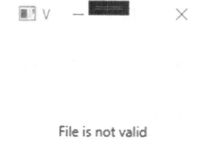

Figure 6-22. *Text displayed when file is invalid*

Once the file is picked, verification will begin automatically. Once complete, the user will either see "File is valid" in green (see Figure 6-21) or "File is not valid" in red (see Figure 6-22).

Figure 6-23. *File layout for the project*

The project contains the main window, two more windows, the model for the saved file, and finally a class for our custom message box (see Figure 6-23).

Listing 6-9. Custom message box class constructor

```
public string OutputText { get; private set; }
        public int OptionClicked { get; private set; }
        private int MessageType;
        public bool InputOK { get; set; }

        private string msg = "";
        private string cp = "";

        /// <summary>
        ///
        /// </summary>
        /// <param name="message"></param>
        /// <param name="caption"></param>
        /// <param name="type">1 - OK, 2 - Yes/No, 3 - Yes/No/
        Cancel, 4 - OK/Cancel</param>
```

```
public FLSMessageBox(string message, string caption,
int type)
{
    msg = message;
    cp = caption;
    MessageType = type;
}
Window win = new Window();
TextBox tb = new TextBox();
```

We will begin with the contents of FLSMessageBox class (Listing 6-9) (FLS – file signature). First, the OutputText variable is public as this is how we can access the inserted text. OptionClicked is set when a specific button is clicked (e.g., OK), and MessageType determines which set of buttons will be displayed. This is similar to the generic message box, but we use integer values to encode things. InputOK is a Boolean value and when set to true will display the text box. After that, we have msg and cp variables – one is the message displayed and the other is caption – or as you will see later, it is a title for the window. With all that, we have a constructor through which we can set the appropriate values. And finally, we have Window and TextBox established.

You should also notice how the constructor method is commented, whenever you do some kind of encoding with integers; you need to note that somewhere in case someone else has to work on it. This way allows others to see what needs to be inserted without having to access the original class.

Listing 6-10. Show method in FLSMessageBox.cs

```
public int Show()
        {
            Grid maingrid = new Grid();
            win.Content = maingrid;
            win.Height = 150;
            win.Width = 300;
            win.ResizeMode = ResizeMode.CanMinimize;
            win.Title = cp;

            //inputbox
            tb.Height = 25;
            tb.Width = 160;
            tb.HorizontalAlignment = HorizontalAlignment.Left;
            tb.VerticalAlignment = VerticalAlignment.Center;
            tb.Margin = new Thickness(0, 0, 0, 0);

            //label
            Label lb = new Label();
            lb.Height = 25;
            lb.Width = 160;
            lb.HorizontalAlignment = HorizontalAlignment.Left;
            lb.VerticalAlignment = VerticalAlignment.Top;
            lb.Margin = new Thickness(0, 0, 0, 0);
            lb.Content = msg;

            //okay
            Button bt_okay = new Button();
            bt_okay.Content = "Ok";
            bt_okay.Height = 25;
            bt_okay.Width = 40;
```

```
bt_okay.HorizontalAlignment = HorizontalAlignment.
Left;
bt_okay.VerticalAlignment = VerticalAlignment.
Bottom;
bt_okay.Margin = new Thickness(0, 0, 0, 0);
bt_okay.Click += Bt_okay_Click;

//yes
Button bt_yes = new Button();
bt_yes.Content = "Yes";
bt_yes.Height = 25;
bt_yes.Width = 40;
bt_yes.HorizontalAlignment = HorizontalAlignment.
Left;
bt_yes.VerticalAlignment = VerticalAlignment.
Bottom;
bt_yes.Margin = new Thickness(40, 0, 0, 0);
bt_yes.Click += Bt_yes_Click;

//no
Button bt_no = new Button();
bt_no.Content = "No";
bt_no.Height = 25;
bt_no.Width = 40;
bt_no.HorizontalAlignment = HorizontalAlignment.
Left;
bt_no.VerticalAlignment = VerticalAlignment.Bottom;
bt_no.Margin = new Thickness(80, 0, 0, 0);
bt_no.Click += Bt_no_Click;

//cancel
Button bt_cancel = new Button();
bt_cancel.Content = "Cancel";
```

```
bt_cancel.Height = 25;
bt_cancel.Width = 40;
bt_cancel.HorizontalAlignment =
HorizontalAlignment.Left;
bt_cancel.VerticalAlignment = VerticalAlignment.
Bottom;
bt_cancel.Margin = new Thickness(120, 0, 0, 0);
bt_cancel.Click += Bt_cancel_Click;

switch (MessageType)
{
    case 1:
        maingrid.Children.Add(bt_okay);
        break;
    case 2:
        maingrid.Children.Add(bt_no);
        maingrid.Children.Add(bt_yes);
        break;
    case 3:
        maingrid.Children.Add(bt_no);
        maingrid.Children.Add(bt_yes);
        maingrid.Children.Add(bt_cancel);
        break;
    case 4:
        maingrid.Children.Add(bt_okay);
        maingrid.Children.Add(bt_cancel);
        break;
    default:
        break;
}

maingrid.Children.Add(lb);
```

```
    if (InputOK)
    {
        maingrid.Children.Add(tb);
    }
    win.ShowDialog();
    return OptionClicked;
}
```

The next part of the class is the Show method (See Listing 6-10); although it is rather large, it is not too complicated. We already have a window established, but every window needs a container, and that is why we need a grid. Once the grid is established, we set it as Content for the window, and we also set some other values for the window. Next, we must deal with the text box – for it, we simply set some values to display it properly in the window. With the text box, we establish a label to display the message.

Once we are done with the text box and other pieces, we need to deal with the buttons. We have four buttons – OK, Yes, No, and Cancel. Every one of them has some text content, some style properties, and then a different event assigned to each method. Once we have these variables defined, we can determine which of them will be displayed. We use switch statement for that according to MessageType, and in each case, we add appropriate buttons to the children list of the grid. Finally, we add label to the children and check for InputOK Boolean to be true; if so, we also add the text box. Once everything is added, we can use the ShowDialog method to display the message box window. It is important to use ShowDialog because we only want to return after the user takes action on one of the buttons.

Listing 6-11. Click events in FLSMessageBox.cs

```csharp
private void Bt_okay_Click(object sender, RoutedEventArgs e)
        {
            if (InputOK)
            {
                OutputText = tb.Text;
            }
            OptionClicked = 1;
            win.Close();
        }

        private void Bt_yes_Click(object sender,
        RoutedEventArgs e)
        {
            if (InputOK)
            {
                OutputText = tb.Text;
            }
            OptionClicked = 2;
            win.Close();
        }

        private void Bt_no_Click(object sender,
        RoutedEventArgs e)
        {
            if (InputOK)
            {
                OutputText = tb.Text;
            }
            OptionClicked = 3;
            win.Close();
        }
```

```
private void Bt_cancel_Click(object sender,
RoutedEventArgs e)
{
    OptionClicked = 4;
    win.Close();
}
```

The final thing in the message box class (See Listing 6-11) will be the events for the buttons. In every event, we first check for InputOK to be true, and if it is, we set the OutputText. With that, we need to set OptionClicked according to which button was clicked, and once the values are set, we can close the window. And once the window is closed, the Show method will continue and return the value.

Listing 6-12. Contents of the main window

```
<Window x:Class="FileSignatureApplication.MainWindow"
        xmlns="http://schemas.microsoft.com/winfx/2006/xaml/
        presentation"
        xmlns:x="http://schemas.microsoft.com/winfx/2006/xaml"
        xmlns:d="http://schemas.microsoft.com/expression/
        blend/2008"
        xmlns:mc="http://schemas.openxmlformats.org/markup-
        compatibility/2006"
        xmlns:local="clr-namespace:FileSignatureApplication"
        mc:Ignorable="d"
        Title="File verifier" Height="450" Width="800">
    <Grid>
        <Button Content="Create signature"
        Style="{DynamicResource GeneralButtonStyle}"
        HorizontalAlignment="Left" Margin="156,187,0,0"
        VerticalAlignment="Top" Width="125" Click="Button_
        Click"/>
```

```
    <Button Content="Verify" Style="{DynamicResource
    GeneralButtonStyle}" HorizontalAlignment="Left"
    Margin="526,187,0,0" VerticalAlignment="Top" Width="75"
    Click="Button_Click_1"/>
  </Grid>
</Window>
```

We will get back to the message box implementation later, but for now, we must look at the style of the buttons (See Listing 6-12). Every button except for the copy button is exactly the same style. They have purple background and a yellowish text. You may notice in the main window we have DynamicResource set in style.

Listing 6-13. Button style template

```
<!-- General button style -->
    <Style x:Key="GeneralButtonStyle" TargetType="{x:Type
    Button}">
        <Setter Property="FocusVisualStyle"
        Value="{StaticResource FocusVisual}"/>
        <Setter Property="Background" Value="#FF322D66"/>
        <Setter Property="BorderBrush" Value="White"/>
        <Setter Property="Foreground" Value="#FFCBCB00"/>
        <Setter Property="BorderThickness" Value="1"/>
        <Setter Property="HorizontalContentAlignment"
        Value="Center"/>
        <Setter Property="VerticalContentAlignment"
        Value="Center"/>
        <Setter Property="Padding" Value="7"/>
        <Setter Property="Template">
            <Setter.Value>
                <ControlTemplate TargetType="{x:Type
                Button}">
```

```xml
<Border x:Name="border" BorderBrush=
"{TemplateBinding BorderBrush}"
BorderThickness="{TemplateBinding
BorderThickness}" Background=
"{TemplateBinding Background}"
SnapsToDevicePixels="true">
    <ContentPresenter
    x:Name="contentPresenter"
    Focusable="False" Horizonta
    lAlignment="{TemplateBindi
    ng HorizontalContentAlignment}"
    Margin="{TemplateBinding Padding}"
    RecognizesAccessKey="True" Snap
    sToDevicePixels="{TemplateBindi
    ng SnapsToDevicePixels}" Verti
    calAlignment="{TemplateBinding
    VerticalContentAlignment}"/>
</Border>
<ControlTemplate.Triggers>
    <Trigger Property="IsDefaulted"
    Value="true">
        <Setter Property="BorderBrush"
        TargetName="border"
        Value="{DynamicResource
        {x:Static SystemColors.
        HighlightBrushKey}}"/>
    </Trigger>
    <Trigger Property="IsMouseOver"
    Value="true">
        <Setter Property="Background"
        TargetName="border"
        Value="#BF322D66"/>
```

```
                        <Setter Property="BorderBrush"
                        TargetName="border"
                        Value="White"/>
                    </Trigger>
                    <Trigger Property="IsPressed"
                    Value="true">
                        <Setter Property="Background"
                        TargetName="border"
                        Value="#BF322D66"/>
                        <Setter Property="BorderBrush"
                        TargetName="border"
                        Value="Transparent"/>
                        <Setter  Property="TextElement.
                        FontSize"
                        TargetName="contentPresenter"
                        Value="13" />
                    </Trigger>
                    <Trigger Property="IsEnabled"
                    Value="false">
                        <Setter Property="Background"
                        TargetName="border"
                        Value="{StaticResource Button.
                        Disabled.Background}"/>
                        <Setter Property="BorderBrush"
                        TargetName="border"
                        Value="{StaticResource Button.
                        Disabled.Border}"/>
                        <Setter Property="TextElement.
                        Foreground"
                        TargetName="contentPresenter"
                        Value="{StaticResource Button.
                        Disabled.Foreground}"/>
```

```
            </Trigger>
        </ControlTemplate.Triggers>
      </ControlTemplate>
    </Setter.Value>
  </Setter>
</Style>
```

In this case, we have the style set in App.xaml (See Listing 6-13). You can see that the style is called GeneralButtonStyle and the target type for it is Button. Initially here, we have some simple properties – background, foreground, and other basic things. But then, to make the button functional, we need something more elaborate. In the ControlTemplate, we have ControlTemplate.Triggers; this is what helps things change on different events. If the Trigger is IsMouseOver, then the background color will change. We also have different values for when the button is clicked.

Listing 6-14. MainWindow.xaml.cs content

```
public MainWindow()
    {
        InitializeComponent();
        var msg = new FLSMessageBox("Pick initial
        directory", "Setup", 2);
        msg.InputOK = true;

        if (msg.Show() == 2)
        {
            App.initialdirectory = msg.OutputText;
        }
    }
```

```
private void Button_Click(object sender,
RoutedEventArgs e)
{
    Window win = new SignatureWindow();

    win.Show();
}

private void Button_Click_1(object sender,
RoutedEventArgs e)
{
    Window win = new VerificationWindow();

    win.Show();
}
```

In the main window (See Listing 6-14), we first need to display the custom message box. To do that, we construct the FLSMessageBox class; we provide the message, caption, and then the type. Also, we must set InputOK to true, as we do need the text box here. If the user clicks the Yes button, we set the output text to a static variable in App.xaml.cs – initialdirectory. With that, we only have a couple of button events which display the appropriate windows.

Listing 6-15. File signature creation window XAML code

```
<Grid>
        <Grid x:Name="InitialGrid" Visibility="Visible"
        HorizontalAlignment="Left" Height="450"
        VerticalAlignment="Top" Width="350"
        Margin="229,0,0,-29">
            <Button x:Name="PickFile_button"
            Style="{DynamicResource GeneralButtonStyle}"
            Content="Pick file" HorizontalAlignment="Left"
            Margin="141,214,0,0" VerticalAlignment="Top"
            Width="75"/>
```

```
</Grid>
<Grid x:Name="PrimaryGrid" Visibility="Hidden"
HorizontalAlignment="Left" Height="411"
Margin="0,0,-6,0" VerticalAlignment="Top" Width="800">
    <Button  x:Name="GenerateSignature_
    button" Content="Generate signature"
    HorizontalAlignment="Left" Margin="359,211,0,0"
    VerticalAlignment="Top" Width="125"
    Style="{DynamicResource GeneralButtonStyle}"/>
    <ProgressBar x:Name="MainProgressBar"
    HorizontalAlignment="Left" Height="5"
    Margin="0,0,0,0" VerticalAlignment="Bottom"
    Width="800">
        <ProgressBar.Foreground>
            <RadialGradientBrush>
                <GradientStop Color="#4C411270"
                Offset="0"/>
                <GradientStop Color="#66410E7E"
                Offset="1"/>
                <GradientStop Color="#FF040008"
                Offset="0.262"/>
                <GradientStop Color="#FF2E095A"
                Offset="0.767"/>
            </RadialGradientBrush>
        </ProgressBar.Foreground>
        <ProgressBar.Background>
            <RadialGradientBrush>
                <GradientStop Color="#FF1B3BFB"
                Offset="1"/>
                <GradientStop Color="#FF3500C3"/>
                <GradientStop Color="#B2500B80"
                Offset="0.56"/>
```

```
                </RadialGradientBrush>
            </ProgressBar.Background>
        </ProgressBar>
        <Label Content="Size:" HorizontalAlignment="Left"
        Margin="568,154,0,0" VerticalAlignment="Top"/>
        <Button  x:Name="OpenFile_button"
        Content="Open file" HorizontalAlignment="Left"
        Margin="359,151,0,0" VerticalAlignment="Top"
        Width="125" Style="{DynamicResource
        GeneralButtonStyle}"/>
        <Label Content="Type:" HorizontalAlignment="Left"
        Margin="568,185,0,0" VerticalAlignment="Top"
        Width="49"/>
        <Label  Content="Name:" HorizontalAlignment="Left"
        Margin="568,214,0,0" VerticalAlignment="Top"
        Width="49"/>
        <Label x:Name="label_filename" Content=""
        HorizontalAlignment="Left" Margin="622,214,0,0"
        VerticalAlignment="Top" Width="146"/>
        <Label x:Name="label_filetype" Content=""
        HorizontalAlignment="Left" Margin="622,185,0,0"
        VerticalAlignment="Top" Width="69"/>
        <Label x:Name="label_filesize" Content=""
        HorizontalAlignment="Left" Margin="622,154,0,0"
        VerticalAlignment="Top" Width="69"/>
        <Grid HorizontalAlignment="Left" Height="100"
        Margin="10,154,0,0" VerticalAlignment="Top"
        Width="310">
            <Button x:Name="Copy_button" Content="Copy"
            HorizontalAlignment="Left" Margin="255,10,0,0"
            VerticalAlignment="Top" Width="37"
            Height="23"/>
```

```
        <TextBox x:Name="OutputBox"
        TextWrapping="NoWrap" IsReadOnly="True"
        HorizontalAlignment="Left" Height="23"
        Margin="10,10,0,0" VerticalAlignment="Top"
        Width="245"/>
        </Grid>
    </Grid>
</Grid>
```

We will now look at the file signature creation arrangement. First, in the XAML (see Listing 6-15), you may notice we have two grids – InitialGrid and PrimaryGrid. Remember, when the user opens this window, they first only see one button – that would be the InitialGrid. Once the file is picked, the InitialGrid gets closed and then the PrimaryGrid is opened. In the PrimaryGrid, we have some simple elements – buttons and labels – but with that, we also have a progress bar and then a text box for the signature to be displayed. The progress bar here is gradient purple; that is why the code for it is rather complex. But all of that, you can simply select in the properties section of visual studio; you do not have to write the code in the XAML. The text box here is quite unusual; it is set to read-only (IsReadOnly) because we only want to display the text. We do it this way because you cannot highlight the text in labels and text blocks.

Listing 6-16. File picker for the signature

```
byte[] SelectedFileBt;
        string FilePath;
        private  void PickFile(object obj, RoutedEventArgs e)
        {
            var dialog = new Microsoft.Win32.OpenFileDialog();
            dialog.InitialDirectory = App.initialdirectory;
```

```
if (dialog.ShowDialog() == true)
{
    string tempname = dialog.FileName;

    var parsedname = tempname.Split('.');

    FileStream selectedfile = (FileStream)dialog.
    OpenFile();

    MemoryStream mstr = new MemoryStream();
    selectedfile.CopyTo(mstr);
    SelectedFileBt = mstr.ToArray();

    FilePath = dialog.FileName;
    label_filename.Content =  (parsedname[0].
    Split('\\')).Last();

    if (selectedfile.Length < 1000000)
    {
        label_filesize.Content = Math.
        Round(Convert.ToDouble(selectedfile.Length)
        / 1024, 0).ToString() + "Kb";
    }

    if (selectedfile.Length >= 1000000 &&
    selectedfile.Length < 10000000)
    {
        label_filesize.Content = Math.Round(Convert.
        ToDouble(selectedfile.Length )/ 1024 /
        1024,2).ToString() + "Mb";
    }
```

```
if (selectedfile.Length >= 10000000)
{
    label_filesize.Content = Math.Round(Convert.
    ToDouble(selectedfile.Length) / 1024 / 1024
    / 1024,2).ToString() + "Gb";
}

label_filetype.Content = parsedname[1];

InitialGrid.Visibility = Visibility.Collapsed;
PrimaryGrid.Visibility = Visibility.Visible;

    }
}
```

To make this a bit more straightforward, we will be using a byte array as the source for the file signature (See Listing 6-16). It is possible to generate it from the FileStream, but that would require an additional byte array for the key and that may overcomplicate our example. Along with the SelectedFileBt byte array, we also have the FilePath string, which will be used for opening files.

In the PickFile event, we start with generic file picking arrangement; after the FilePath is set, the more specific arrangement begins. We split the file name and set it to Content of label_filename to display it. After that, we have what may seem like a very complex arrangement, but this is only to display the size properly. The initial value we get is in bytes, which would be a huge number for most files; that is why we use if statements, and on certain intervals, we display it either in kilobytes, megabytes, or even gigabytes. Once the size is displayed, we set Content of label_filetype to display the extension. And then once everything is displayed, we close the InitialGrid and open the PrimaryGrid.

Listing 6-17. CreateSignature method

```
byte[] Signature;
        public async void CreateSignature(object obj,
        RoutedEventArgs e)
        {
            ((Button)obj).IsEnabled = false;
            MainProgressBar.IsIndeterminate = true;
            await Task.Run(() =>
            {
                var hasher = new System.Security.Cryptography.
                HMACSHA512(SelectedFileBt);

                Signature = hasher.ComputeHash(SelectedFileBt);

                Dispatcher.Invoke(() => {
                    SaveRecord();
                    OutputBox.Text = Convert.
                    ToBase64String(Signature);
                    ((Button)obj).IsEnabled = true;

                    MainProgressBar.IsIndeterminate = false;
                });

            });

        }
```

After the file is picked, we need to deal with the signature (See
Listing 6-17). It will be a byte array, and that is why we have the Signature
variable declared. The CreateSignature event occurs when the "Create
signature" button is clicked, and in it, we first disable the button so
that it would not be clicked again. We also set the MainProgressBar as
indeterminate. We run the whole thing on a background thread, and to
create the signature (or the hash as that is what it is), we use HMACSHA512

from System.Security.Cryptography. In the constructor, it takes a key, and then in the ComputeHash, it takes the data that needs to be hashed. As mentioned previously, we simplify this by providing key as the file itself. For the output to be matching, the key has to match as well as the data (in this case, file) provided. Since we are in a different thread at this point, we need to use Dispatcher.Invoke to access the elements in the UI. You may also notice the SaveRecord method; this is to save the file signature for later verification; we will cover that next.

Listing 6-18. SaveFileModel class

```
[Serializable]
    public class SaveFileModel
    {
        public  DateTime LastSaved { get; set; }
        public List<byte[]> Signatures { get; set; } = new
        List<byte[]>();
    }
```

Listing 6-19. SaveRecord method

```
public void SaveRecord()
        {
            var formatter = new System.Runtime.Serialization.
            Formatters.Binary.BinaryFormatter();
             FileStream savefile = File.Create(Environment.
            GetFolderPath(Environment.SpecialFolder.
            MyDocuments) + "\\savefile.fsappsf");
            App.currentsavedata.Signatures.Add(Signature);
            formatter.Serialize(savefile, App.currentsavedata);
        }
```

We keep the signatures in a file as a simple list (Listing 6-19). The file is basically a serialized data model (See Listing 6-18) object. In it, we have the date which states when was the time it was saved and then the list for the byte arrays (signatures). To achieve this, we want to serialize the class object to a byte array and then save that data to a file. For it, we use BinaryFormatter, and we simply serialize that into the FileStream itself. You may notice the extension for the savefile is fsappsf, which is our custom format.

Listing 6-20. Events for signature creation window

```
public void OpenFile(object obj, RoutedEventArgs e)
        {
            System.Diagnostics.Process.Start(FilePath);
        }

        public void CopyToClipboard(object obj,
        RoutedEventArgs e)
        {
            Clipboard.SetText(OutputBox.Text);
        }
```

With all that, we have couple more events in the window (See Listing 6-20). The OpenFile event will use Process.Start to basically open the file from the file path provided. Then the CopyToClipboard will set the text in the clipboard from the output box.

```
protected override void OnClosing(CancelEventArgs e)
        {
            if (MainProgressBar.IsIndeterminate)
            {
                var msg = MessageBox.Show("Signature is being
                created, are you sure you want to exit?","ready
                to leave?",MessageBoxButton.OKCancel);
```

```
        if (msg == MessageBoxResult.Cancel)
        {
            e.Cancel = true;
        }
    }
    base.OnClosing(e);
}
```

Finally, we have a little notification if the user attempts to close the window while the signature is being generated. We simply check for the MainProgressBar to be IsIndeterminate, and if true, we display a message box. You have seen similar arrangements previously, but this case implements additional variable for this.

Listing 6-21. XAML code for the verification window

```
<Grid>
        <Grid x:Name="initialgrid"    HorizontalAlignment="Left"
        Height="136" Margin="10,48,0,0" VerticalAlignment="Top"
        Width="156">
            <Button x:Name="PickFile_button"
            Style="{DynamicResource GeneralButtonStyle}"
            Click="PickFile_button_Click" Content="Pick
            and verify" HorizontalAlignment="Left"
            Margin="21,58,0,0" VerticalAlignment="Top"
            Width="102"/>
        </Grid>
        <Grid x:Name="resultgrid" Visibility="Hidden"
        HorizontalAlignment="Left" Height="136"
        Margin="10,48,0,0" VerticalAlignment="Top" Width="156">
```

```
<Label x:Name="validlabel" Content="File is valid"
HorizontalAlignment="Left" Margin="29,43,0,0"
VerticalAlignment="Top" Width="102"
Foreground="#FF2DA400"/>
<Label x:Name="notvalidlabel" Content="File
is not valid" HorizontalAlignment="Left"
Margin="29,25,0,0" VerticalAlignment="Top"
Width="102" Foreground="#FFBF0000"/>
</Grid>
<ProgressBar x:Name="MainProgressBar"
Visibility="Hidden"  HorizontalAlignment="Left"
Height="6" Margin="0,0,0,100"
VerticalAlignment="Bottom" Width="185">
    <ProgressBar.Foreground>
        <RadialGradientBrush>
            <GradientStop Color="#4C411270"
            Offset="0"/>
            <GradientStop Color="#66410E7E"
            Offset="1"/>
            <GradientStop Color="#FF040008"
            Offset="0.262"/>
            <GradientStop Color="#FF2E095A"
            Offset="0.767"/>
        </RadialGradientBrush>
    </ProgressBar.Foreground>
    <ProgressBar.Background>
        <RadialGradientBrush>
            <GradientStop Color="#FF1B3BFB"
            Offset="1"/>
            <GradientStop Color="#FF3500C3"/>
            <GradientStop Color="#B2500B80"
            Offset="0.56"/>
```

```
        </RadialGradientBrush>
      </ProgressBar.Background>
    </ProgressBar>
</Grid>
```

The verification window layout is in a way similar to signature creation (See Listing 6-21). We first have initial grid, and only after the file is picked, the resultgrid will open up. The resultgrid contains couple of different labels for the two different outcomes and a progress bar.

Listing 6-22. Contents for App.xaml.cs

```
public partial class App : Application
    {
        public static SaveFileModel currentsavedata = new
        SaveFileModel();

        public static string initialdirectory = "D:\\test";
        protected override void OnStartup(StartupEventArgs e)
        {
            var formatter = new System.Runtime.Serialization.
            Formatters.Binary.BinaryFormatter();

            FileStream savefile = File.OpenRead(Environment.
            GetFolderPath(Environment.SpecialFolder.
            MyDocuments) + "\\savefile.fsappsf");

            var savedata =  formatter.Deserialize(savefile);
            currentsavedata = (SaveFileModel)savedata;

            base.OnStartup(e);
        }
    }
```

Before we get into the verification process in C#, we first need to take a look at App.xaml.cs (See Listing 6-22) to see how the saved data is retrieved and set up for use. You can see the initialdirectory static string, which we set in the MainWindow from the custom message box. With that, you can see currentsavedata, which is where we have our signatures ready for use. When the application starts, we retrieve the data from the save file and set it to that variable.

Listing 6-23. File picker event for verification

```
private async void PickFile_button_Click(object sender,
RoutedEventArgs e)
    {
        initialgrid.Visibility = Visibility.Hidden;
        MainProgressBar.IsIndeterminate = true;
        MainProgressBar.Visibility = Visibility.Visible;

        var dialog = new Microsoft.Win32.OpenFileDialog();
        dialog.InitialDirectory = "D:\\test";
        if (dialog.ShowDialog() == true)
        {
            string tempname = dialog.FileName;
            FileStream selectedfile = (FileStream)dialog.
            OpenFile();

            await Task.Run(() =>
            {
                MemoryStream mstr = new MemoryStream();
                selectedfile.CopyTo(mstr);
                byte[] SelectedFileBt = mstr.ToArray();

                var hasher = new System.Security.
                Cryptography.HMACSHA512(SelectedFileBt);
```

```
byte[] signature = hasher.
ComputeHash(SelectedFileBt);

Dispatcher.Invoke(() => {
    if (App.currentsavedata.Signatures.
    Exists(x => Convert.ToBase64String(x)
    ==  Convert.ToBase64String(signature)))
    {
        validlabel.Visibility = Visibility.
        Visible;
        notvalidlabel.Visibility =
        Visibility.Hidden;
    }
    else
    {
        notvalidlabel.Visibility =
        Visibility.Visible;
        validlabel.Visibility = Visibility.
        Hidden;
    }
    MainProgressBar.IsIndeterminate =
    false;
    MainProgressBar.Visibility =
    Visibility.Hidden;
    resultgrid.Visibility = Visibility.
    Visible;
    });

    });
}
}
```

In the verification window, everything happens on one single event (See Listing 6-23). Once the button is clicked, the operation begins, and we have to hide the initial grid as well as turn on the progress bar. After that, the file dialog opens, and the user can pick the file. After we retrieve the file, we once again start a background task and do the hard work in there. To verify the file, we need to generate the same kind of signature for that provided file. After that, we simply check if the signature exists in the list and display the result. Once again, it is important to note that we have to use the Dispatcher.Invoke method (refer to Chapter 3 "Background Tasks" section).

Quick Exercise

Your task is to create a basic drawing application that allows the user to draw on specified canvas area. There is no ability to save the drawing or export an image.

The images for the layout (see Figures 6-24 to 6-27) and some accessories are provided; these are from the example solution, but you may treat them as a mockup template. The features should be created according to the layout image.

The style for the button are as follows:

- The buttons should have no border.

- The buttons should have the default background.

- The buttons should have the default color and size for the text.

- When a button is hovered on, a border should appear.

- When a button is clicked, it should retain the border and the text size should be smaller.

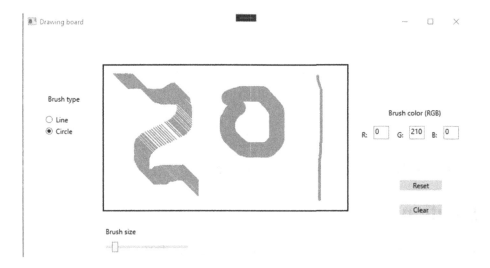

Figure 6-24. *View for the exercise window*

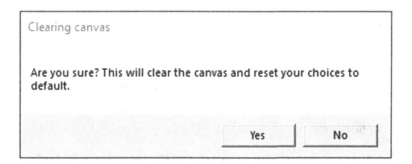

Figure 6-25. *"reset" button click notification*

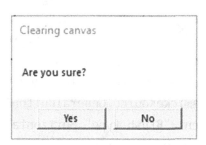

Figure 6-26. *"clear" button click notification*

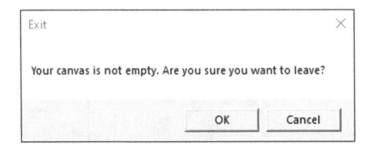

Figure 6-27. *Notification before closing*

Solution

Listing 6-24. XAML code for the example window

```
<Grid>
        <Border BorderBrush="Black" BorderThickness="2"
        Margin="141,58,212,98">
            <Canvas MouseMove="canv_MouseMove"
            Background="White"  x:Name="canv"
            HorizontalAlignment="Left" Height="251"
            VerticalAlignment="Top" Width="427"/>
        </Border>

        <Button x:Name="bt_clear" Click="bt_clear_Click"
        Content="Clear" HorizontalAlignment="Left"
        Margin="661,301,0,0" VerticalAlignment="Top" Width="75"
        Style="{DynamicResource GeneralButtonStyle}"/>
        <Button x:Name="bt_reset" Click="bt_reset_Click"
        Content="Reset" HorizontalAlignment="Left"
        Margin="661,259,0,0" VerticalAlignment="Top" Width="75"
        Style="{DynamicResource GeneralButtonStyle}"/>
        <Label Content="Brush type" HorizontalAlignment="Left"
        Margin="39,105,0,0" VerticalAlignment="Top"/>
```

```
<RadioButton x:Name="rb_brushtype1" Content="Line"
GroupName="brushtype" HorizontalAlignment="Left"
Margin="39,147,0,0" VerticalAlignment="Top"/>
<RadioButton x:Name="rb_brushtype2" IsChecked="True"
Content="Circle" GroupName="brushtype"
HorizontalAlignment="Left" Margin="39,167,0,0"
VerticalAlignment="Top"/>
<Slider x:Name="slider_brushsize"
HorizontalAlignment="Left" Margin="141,366,0,0"
VerticalAlignment="Top" Width="154"/>
<Label Content="Brush size" HorizontalAlignment="Left"
Margin="141,335,0,0" VerticalAlignment="Top"/>
<TextBox x:Name="tb_color_r" Text="0"
HorizontalAlignment="Left" Height="23"
Margin="616,165,0,0" TextWrapping="Wrap"
VerticalAlignment="Top" Width="27"/>
<TextBox x:Name="tb_color_g" Text="0"
HorizontalAlignment="Left" Height="23"
Margin="678,165,0,0" TextWrapping="Wrap"
VerticalAlignment="Top" Width="27"/>
<TextBox x:Name="tb_color_b" Text="0"
HorizontalAlignment="Left" Height="23"
Margin="739,165,0,0" TextWrapping="Wrap"
VerticalAlignment="Top" Width="27"/>
<Label Content="R:" HorizontalAlignment="Left"
Margin="590,167,0,0" VerticalAlignment="Top"
Width="26"/>
<Label Content="G:" HorizontalAlignment="Left"
Margin="652,167,0,0" VerticalAlignment="Top"
Width="26"/>
```

```
<Label Content="B:" HorizontalAlignment="Left"
Margin="713,167,0,0" VerticalAlignment="Top"
Width="26"/>
<Label Content="Brush color (RGB)"
HorizontalAlignment="Left" Margin="637,129,0,0"
VerticalAlignment="Top"/>
</Grid>
```

We should first look at the Grid for the window (See Listing 6-24), which is quite complex in this case. But first, the main thing here is the canvas, and it does not have a border in itself. The canvas itself has a fixed size and event and the name for it. After that, we have the two buttons you see in the window – they have appropriate events and then style templates applied. Then, we get to radio buttons for brush type – we have proper names (starting with **rb**) and a group name, as only one can be selected at a time. After that, we have a Slider; it has a name, but to get rid of any possible confusion, we will set the values (minimum, maximum, and current) later in the C# code. With all that, you can see three small text boxes and three labels for our primitive color RGB color picker.

Since we have a lot of elements, proper naming system is a must here. You may notice that we use tb for text box, bt for button, and so on. This way, if you look for some button in the C# code, you can simply type in bt and the IntelliSense will suggest all the choices.

Listing 6-25. Template for the buttons

```
<Window.Resources>
        <Style x:Key="FocusVisual">
            <Setter Property="Control.Template">
                <Setter.Value>
```

```
        <ControlTemplate>
            <Rectangle Margin="2"
            SnapsToDevicePixels="true"
            Stroke="{DynamicResource {x:Static
            SystemColors.ControlTextBrushKey}}"
            StrokeThickness="1" StrokeDashArray="1
            2"/>
        </ControlTemplate>
    </Setter.Value>
    </Setter>
</Style>
<SolidColorBrush x:Key="Button.Static.Background"
Color="#FFDDDDDD"/>
<SolidColorBrush x:Key="Button.Static.Border"
Color="#FF707070"/>
<SolidColorBrush x:Key="Button.MouseOver.Background"
Color="#FFBEE6FD"/>
<SolidColorBrush x:Key="Button.MouseOver.Border"
Color="#FF3C7FB1"/>
<SolidColorBrush x:Key="Button.Pressed.Background"
Color="#FFC4E5F6"/>
<SolidColorBrush x:Key="Button.Pressed.Border"
Color="#FF2C628B"/>
<SolidColorBrush x:Key="Button.Disabled.Background"
Color="#FFF4F4F4"/>
<SolidColorBrush x:Key="Button.Disabled.Border"
Color="#FFADB2B5"/>
<SolidColorBrush x:Key="Button.Disabled.Foreground"
Color="#FF838383"/>
<Style x:Key="GeneralButtonStyle" TargetType="{x:Type
Button}">
```

```xml
<Setter Property="FocusVisualStyle"
Value="{StaticResource FocusVisual}"/>
<Setter Property="Background"
Value="{StaticResource Button.Static.Background}"/>
<Setter Property="BorderBrush"
Value="{StaticResource Button.Static.Border}"/>
<Setter Property="Foreground"
Value="{DynamicResource {x:Static SystemColors.
ControlTextBrushKey}}"/>
<Setter Property="BorderThickness" Value="0"/>
<Setter Property="HorizontalContentAlignment"
Value="Center"/>
<Setter Property="VerticalContentAlignment"
Value="Center"/>
<Setter Property="Padding" Value="1"/>
<Setter Property="Template">
    <Setter.Value>
        <ControlTemplate TargetType="{x:Type
        Button}">
            <Border x:Name="border"
            BorderBrush="{TemplateBinding
            BorderBrush}" BorderThickness="{T
            emplateBinding BorderThickness}"
            Background="{TemplateBinding
            Background}"
            SnapsToDevicePixels="true">
                <ContentPresenter
                x:Name="contentPresenter"
                Focusable="False"
                HorizontalAlignment="{Template
                Binding HorizontalContent
```

```xml
            Alignment}" Margin="{Template
            Binding Padding}" Recognizes
            AccessKey="True" SnapsToDevice
            Pixels="{TemplateBinding
            SnapsToDevicePixels}" Vertical
            Alignment="{TemplateBinding
            VerticalContentAlignment}"/>
        </Border>
        <ControlTemplate.Triggers>
            <Trigger Property="IsDefaulted"
            Value="true">
                <Setter Property="BorderBrush"
                TargetName="border"
                Value="{DynamicResource
                {x:Static SystemColors.
                HighlightBrushKey}}"/>
            </Trigger>
            <Trigger Property="IsMouseOver"
            Value="true">
                <Setter Property="Background"
                TargetName="border"
                Value="{StaticResource Button.
                MouseOver.Background}"/>
                <Setter Property="BorderBrush"
                TargetName="border"
                Value="{StaticResource Button.
                MouseOver.Border}"/>
            </Trigger>
            <Trigger Property="IsPressed"
            Value="true">
```

```xml
                            <Setter Property="Background"
                            TargetName="border"
                            Value="{StaticResource Button.
                            Pressed.Background}"/>
                            <Setter Property="BorderBrush"
                            TargetName="border"
                            Value="{StaticResource Button.
                            Pressed.Border}"/>
                        </Trigger>
                        <Trigger Property="IsEnabled"
                        Value="false">
                            <Setter Property="Background"
                            TargetName="border"
                            Value="{StaticResource Button.
                            Disabled.Background}"/>
                            <Setter Property="BorderBrush"
                            TargetName="border"
                            Value="{StaticResource Button.
                            Disabled.Border}"/>
                            <Setter Property="TextElement.
                            Foreground"
                            TargetName="contentPresenter"
                            Value="{StaticResource Button.
                            Disabled.Foreground}"/>
                        </Trigger>
                    </ControlTemplate.Triggers>
                </ControlTemplate>
            </Setter.Value>
        </Setter>
```

```
    <Style.Triggers>
        <Trigger Property="IsPressed" Value="True"  >
            <Setter Property="BorderThickness" Value="2"/>
            <Setter Property="FontSize" Value="10"/>
        </Trigger>
        <Trigger Property="IsMouseOver" Value="True"  >
            <Setter Property="BorderThickness" Value="2"/>
        </Trigger>
    </Style.Triggers>
  </Style>
</Window.Resources>
```

Now that you know what we have in the grid, we can look at that style template for the buttons (See Listing 6-25). When you create your template as a copy, you will get a lot of code, but remember, most of it is just noise that you have to cancel out. In this case, you need to get down to the second Style where you have your key and control type (element type). For your task, you had to set some properties and then set some more properties for specific triggers. Initially, we have BorderThickness set to 0, in other words, no border. Besides that, everything stays as default until we get to the triggers. Here, we need to establish two setups for two types of triggers – IsPressed (when button is clicked) and IsMouseOver (when the button is hovered on). On IsPressed, we set BorderThickness to 2 (making the border appear) and FontSize to 10 (making it smaller than the default). On IsMouseOver, we only need to set BorderThickness to 2, so that the border would be displayed.

Listing 6-26. Mouse move event

```
private void canv_MouseMove(object sender, MouseEventArgs e)
    {
        if (e.LeftButton == MouseButtonState.Pressed)
        {
            if (rb_brushtype1.IsChecked == true)
            {
                Line line = new Line();
                line.Stroke = new SolidColorBrush(Color.
                FromRgb(Convert.ToByte(tb_color_r.Text),
                Convert.ToByte(tb_color_g.Text), Convert.
                ToByte(tb_color_b.Text)));
                line.X1 = e.GetPosition(canv).X;
                line.Y1 = e.GetPosition(canv).Y;
                line.X2 = e.GetPosition(canv).X + slider_
                brushsize.Value;
                line.Y2 = e.GetPosition(canv).Y + slider_
                brushsize.Value;

                canv.Children.Add(line);
            }

            if (rb_brushtype2.IsChecked == true)
            {
                Ellipse ellipse = new Ellipse();
                ellipse.Stroke = new SolidColorBrush(Color.
                FromRgb(Convert.ToByte(tb_color_r.Text),
                Convert.ToByte(tb_color_g.Text), Convert.
                ToByte(tb_color_b.Text)));
```

```
ellipse.Margin = new Thickness(e.
GetPosition(canv).X, e.GetPosition(canv).Y,
e.GetPosition(canv).X + 1,
e.GetPosition(canv).Y + 1);
ellipse.Height = slider_brushsize.Value;
ellipse.Width = slider_brushsize.Value;
ellipse.Fill = new SolidColorBrush(Color.
FromRgb(Convert.ToByte(tb_color_r.Text),
Convert.ToByte(tb_color_g.Text), Convert.
ToByte(tb_color_b.Text)));

                canv.Children.Add(ellipse);
            }

        }
    }
```

Now that you have seen the layout and the styles, we can get to where the action is, and that is the C# part (See Listing 6-26). We will first look at the main event – the MouseMove event relative to the canvas. Initially, we check for the left mouse button to be clicked, and if it is, we are drawing. Inside that, we have another split – two brush types (line and circle); these are determined by radio button values, and that is what we check for. If the line type is selected, we need to construct a new Line object; we also need to add some properties to it. First, we get the Stroke which is the color of the line, and we take values from our RGB color picker. Now, a line has two points, and in this case, the first one will be the coordinates for the mouse and the other will be coordinated plus the size of the brush or, in this case, the length of the line. Once everything is set, we simply add the new Line object to the Children list of the canvas.

The second option is the circle, or in C#, the Ellipse type. This is a bit complex than a line, but not too much to handle. First, we need to establish the object; then we can set the values. Initially, we set Stroke with the provided color arrangement, but if you look at the last property, we also need to set Fill as that color; otherwise, it will be a transparent circle. The Margin in this case will be the position in the canvas; just like the line brush, we move each new element by 1. Finally, we have a Height and a Width, which determine the size of the brush, and they have to match; otherwise, it will not be a circle anymore. And once it is all done, we can add it to the children.

Listing 6-27. Event for "clear" button

```
private void bt_clear_Click(object sender, RoutedEventArgs e)
      {
          if (MessageBox.Show("Are you sure?",
          "Clearing canvas", MessageBoxButton.YesNo) ==
          MessageBoxResult.Yes)
          {
              canv.Children.Clear();
          }

      }
```

To clear the canvas, you simply need to clear the Children list (See Listing 6-27). But before that, we must notify the user as asked in the task. For that, we use simple message box, and if the return is of type Yes, we move forward.

Listing 6-28. Event for "reset" button

```
private void bt_reset_Click(object sender, RoutedEventArgs e)
      {
          if (MessageBox.Show("Are you sure? This will clear
          the canvas and reset your choices to default.",
          "Clearing canvas", MessageBoxButton.YesNo) ==
          MessageBoxResult.Yes)
```

```
        {
            canv.Children.Clear();
            rb_brushtype2.IsChecked = true;
            slider_brushsize.Value = 10;
            tb_color_r.Text = "0";
            tb_color_g.Text = "0";
            tb_color_b.Text = "0";
        }
    }
```

The reset event is a bit more complex than the clear one, but it is still quite straightforward (See Listing 6-28). We notify the user, then we clear the canvas, and finally we set the values of elements to their original state.

Listing 6-29. OnClosing event for the window

```
protected override void OnClosing(CancelEventArgs e)
        {
            if (canv.Children.Count > 0)
            {
                if (MessageBox.Show("Your canvas is not empty.
                Are you sure you want to leave?", "Exit",
                MessageBoxButton.OKCancel) == MessageBoxResult.
                Cancel)
                {
                    e.Cancel = true;
                }
            }

            base.OnClosing(e);
        }
```

Finally, we need to notify the user before closing the window, but only if the canvas is not empty. To do that, we use the OnClosing window event (See Listing 6-29) and check for the Count (of Children list) to be more than 0; if something exists, that means the canvas is not empty anymore, and we have to notify the user.

Index

A

AcceptsReturn property, 13

B

BorderThickness, 217
bt_copy_Click event, 22
bt_generate_Click event, 22
Button and click event
    elements, 1
    file layout, 2
    MainWindow.xaml, 3, 4
    TextBlock, 5
    toolbox, 3
    windows view, 3
Button style, 208, 210

C

CanMinimize, 157
CopyToClipboard, 202
Country data model, 120, 122
CreateSignature method, 200

D

Dispatcher.Invoke method, 83, 208
DrawImage method, 93
DynamicResource set, 190

E

Events
    application, 33, 34
    example, 41–44
    exercise, 44, 45, 47, 48, 50
    keyboard, 38
    mouse, 34, 36–38
    window, 39, 41

F, G, H

File layout, 141, 152, 182
File picker, 86
    button event, 87
    click event, 86
    dialog, 87
    event for verification, 206
    file dialog, 97
    filter, 89
    initial setup, 97
    window view, 96
    XAML code, 90
File signature creation
    arrangement, 197
File verification
    application, 177
FLSMessageBox
    class, 182, 194

I

ImageResizer class, 91, 93, 95
InitalizeComponent method, 11, 41
InputOK Boolean, 187
IsChecked property, 62
IsIndeterminate property, 53

J, K, L

Json-related methods, 126

M, N

MainViewModel class, 107
MainWindow layout, 152
Message box, 14–16
MouseButtonEventArgs event, 36
MouseMove event, 43, 218
MouseRightButtonDown event, 36
MVVM
    API access, 123
    API documentation, 119
    basic encoder, 117
    basic representation, 101
    binding, 103
    C# code, 109
    complex representation, 102
    encoder, 130
    EncoderViewModel, 128
    file layout, 110, 120, 141
    ListView, 110
    lookup feature, 147
    lookup window, 138

OnStartup event, 142
PostAsJsonAsync, 134
product window, 137
verification feature, 118
ViewModel, 104, 105
WPF application, 116
XAML code, 108, 114

O

OnClosing event, 50, 221
OptionClicked, 183, 189
optionMark, 175

P, Q

PickFile event, 199
Properties section, 161

R

ResizeMode, 157
Resource dictionary file
        selection, 176
RGB color picker, 212

S

SaveFileDialog method, 88
SaveRecord method, 201
Scroll viewer, 155
SelectedFileBt byte array, 199
SelectedItem property, 74
Serialized data model, 202

Show method, 8, 17

ShowDialog method, 187

Signature creation window, 179

Style template, 177

T

Task method, 126

tb_password text property, 22

Template setup, 163

TextBlock element, 12, 13, 27, 160

this.Close() method, 8

Triggers, 167

U

UI elements

C#, 78–80

canvas, 75–78

check box, 59–61

image, 64

list view, 71–74

media element, 65–69

menu, 70

progress bar, 51–54

radio button, 56, 57

slider, 62, 63

tabs, 55, 56

web browser, 74, 75

V

ValueChanged event, 63, 69

Verification window

signature creation, 205

XAML code, 203

W

Window and page

adding Window file, 7

constructor method,
Page1, 11

containers, 6

events, 11

file layout, 9

first state view, 9

MainWindow.xaml
contents, 10

second state view, 10

Windows Presentation
Foundation (WPF), 1

example, 18–22

exercise, 22–31

Window template, 166

X, Y, Z

XAML arrangement, 85

Printed in the United States
By Bookmasters